DIMINISHED DREAMS
_____

Printed in the United States of America
First Printing, 2017

ISBN: 978-0-9989702-7-1

Copyright © 2017 by Shelby Bentil

All rights reserved. No part of this publication may be reproduced, distributed, or transmitted in any form or by any means, including photocopying, recording, or other electronic or mechanical methods, without the prior written permission of the publisher, except in the case of brief quotations embodied in critical reviews and certain other noncommercial uses permitted by copyright law. For permission requests, write to the publisher, addressed "Attention: Permissions Coordinator," at the address below.

13th & Joan
500 N. Michigan Ave
Suite #600
Chicago, IL 60611

WWW.13THANDJOAN.COM

TABLE OF CONTENTS

Preface 9
First Bone to the Skeleton 11
Best Friends and Boyfriends 31
Trembling Castle 41
Quickly Slipping 51
Misguided Love 57
Sentiment 69
Hidden Skeleton 79
Betrayal 87
Exposed 95
Crushed Bones 109
Self Destruction 121
The Fallen King 133
A Cry for Help 143
Reality 155
Diminished 163
Conclusion 175
Through the Pain 177
About the Author 181
Connect with Shelby Bentil 183

ACKNOWLEDGEMENTS

To my eldest sister, my twin, Diana. Grateful I am that God blessed you with such artistic talent. Thank you for your amazing support throughout this journey. From reading my draft three years ago to creating the jaw-dropping cover. I am truly appreciative.

Love,
Shelby

To the greatest mother a young woman could ever ask for. You are my entire backbone. Your sacrifice, support and prayers is why I am who I am today. God told you I would be great and you never gave up on me. I am blessed to be your youngest daughter. This is for you!!

With Love,
Akua Mansa

DIMINISHED DREAMS

SHELBY BENTIL

PREFACE

It is a dream come true to see my once high school assignment finally become my very first book. After eight years of writing *Diminished Dreams*, I truly fell in love with how I incorporated my own personal growth and lessons into my characters. When I first wrote the story, the message was fixated on revenge and pain. As I've grown and the years have passed, the focus within the story has been manipulated to bring out the strength and healing within my characters. This difference makes me even more excited to introduce the book to my readers. It is my hope that through the characters and personal stories of Castel, Cherry, Dante, and Josh, you are able to learn and understand who I am and what I went through as a teenager.

"*I did then what I knew how to do. Now that I know better, I do better.*"

— Dr. Maya Angelou

FIRST BONE TO THE SKELETON

"Of all the days you should be giving me a lecture, today is not one of them. Coach went in on me today. You're supposed to be asking me what I want." Dante threw his football stuff across the floor as he kicked off his shoes, his girlfriend Castel following behind him.

"Lecturing? Why is my advice always a lecture to you? And what do you mean, get what you want? Dante don't play with me!" Castel smacked him on the back of the neck.

It was the last week of July and Dante was finally finished with football camp. His girlfriend of three years, Castel, came to meet him at his house.

"The entire team is depending on you this season. You know that. Especially with the majority of the team being in their senior year and the scouts are already hawking around.

You guys need a perfect season." Castel reminded him with seriousness in her voice.

"Yeah, yeah, yeah." Dante shut her down.

Castel got annoyed and rolled her eyes. She hated when Dante didn't take her opinions about his football career seriously. It made her feel like he thought she was only a pretty face. She turned her attention to flexing and stretching her toes.

Dante caught the silence in the air and looked at Castel as she moved her toes back and forth. After the week he had, he was in no mood for the emotions. Dante let out an annoyed sigh and moved to the end of his bed. "Yo? What's the problem?" he asked, snapping his fingers.

Castel looked up with an attitude and then looked back down at her toes. Dante sat up and tossed his basketball at her head, but it missed her by an inch. "Don't play with me!" Castel hissed.

"What's wrong? You always want to get an attitude over nothing."

"I was just giving you a little pep talk, like a good girlfriend. It would be nice if you listened instead of just blowing me off." She folded her arms and pulled her legs toward her.

Dante dropped his head back. He wanted to get up and leave Castel to wallow by herself, but he knew that wouldn't help. He got off his bed and crawled to her. She tried as hard as possible to act as if she was still upset. Dante playfully bit her knee and then rested his chin on it. Castel slowly turned her head towards his. His bright eyes stroked her face and she felt a tingle cover her body.

"I know you got my back Cas. I know and I appreciate it. I wasn't trying to shut down your little opinion, but I'm home, I'm tired, and I got my girl with me." Dante expressed sitting up with his hands out. "The last thing I need right now is to talk about football. Can we puh-lease focus on us and catch up on some quality time?" he begged.

Castel looked back down and then looked up at Dante with a smile. He smiled back and got off the ground. He helped Castel up and led her to the bed. She stretched out in the middle of it as Dante walked over to his stereo system and turned on some soft 90's R&B, turning the volume on high. He went back to his bed and plopped himself next to Castel. He rolled over on top of her and ran his fingers through her hair. He worked his hands down her body and caressed her thighs and gently kissed Castel's full lips. She pulled herself back and looked into Dante's eyes.

"You know we can't," she said softly. Dante looked confused. It was far from the first time they were intimate.

"Your girl visiting or something?" he chuckled.

Castel sucked her teeth. "No fool... your dad. After the last time, I'm not trying to have Brian spaz on me again. It took me a whole week to get my nerves right again after he tried to throw me down the steps," Castel confessed. She tried to move herself from under Dante, but he refused to let her escape.

"Will you relax. He's out doing his club rounds and that always takes him all day. By the time you leave, he won't even know you were here," Dante assured her as he gave her a small peck.

Castel moved her head once again, but this time Dante became annoyed.

"Are you serious right now?"

"Very! You know better than I do what your father is capable of and I'm not trying to end up in pieces."

Dante scoffed. "I just said he won't be home until late! Are you really going to focus on my dad or are you going to show me how much you missed me?"

Castel hesitated. She desperately wanted her quality time with Dante right now, but she feared another run in with Brian. Brian was known for his disgusting temper and the last time he caught Dante and her in the house, she thought she would lose her life.

She let out a deep exhale and jumped out of her thoughts. She wrapped her long legs around him, stroking the middle of his back with her fingertips. Lost in one another, the two of them blocked out the world around them.

Just outside, Dante's father, Brian, pulled in the driveway in his Bentley coupe. "My whole day ruined because of idiots," Brian said out loud. A drug bust near one of his clubs had stopped him from doing his rounds. The police blocked off multiple streets and the last thing Brian needed was to be questioned by police simply because he wanted to get to his own business. He got out his car, aggressively slamming the door and walked up the driveway toward the house. As he entered, he paused at the sound of music blasting from upstairs. He sucked his teeth. "How many times do I have to tell this boy about this music?" Brian grumbled under his breath. "If I got robbed he would be oblivious to the whole thing!" he shouted, as he slightly slammed the front door behind him.

He threw his keys on the table and walked upstairs to make his way to Dante's room. On the steps Brian noticed a pair of Chanel sandals that clearly belonged to a woman. He paused, leaning on the wall and shook his head as he realized his son was doing more than playing loud music. He continued upstairs, stomping harder with each step. He got closer to the room and put his ear to the door. Sounds of soft moans leaked from his son's room over the music. Brian's heart began to race from frustration. He warned Dante on multiple occasions about his little chill dates in his house. Their many arguments began with him reminding Dante their home wasn't a hotel, after catching Dante trying to sneak girls out of the house.

Brian banged on the door with all the strength his arm could give him. A startled Dante lost his balanced and almost crushed Castel's petite frame under him. The two maneuvered to gain their composure as Brian continued to bang on the door.

"Dante!" Brian screamed. "Open this door boy! I know you're not in my house laid up AGAIN? What do I keep telling you about these chicks in my house?" Brian roared over the music.

Castel paused from putting her pants on and turned her attention to Dante. "Chicks? What chicks? So you're cheating? Is that it?" she asked in disgust.

"That's your concern right now?" Dante asked her with a look of confusion on his face as he fumbled to put his shirt on. "Just keep getting dressed!" he ordered.

Castel scoffed and buttoned her pants, then quickly threw on her shirt and ran into the corner out of the way as Dante finally went to open the door. Brian's six foot five muscular frame took up the entire doorway. His face was filled with rage, his fist balled up, and his teeth clenched. He looked passed Dante to Castel, who was in the corner trembling. He slowly turned his head back to Dante who spoke.

"What's up Dad? What's wrong?" Dante asked, playing stupid.

With one swift movement, Brian grabbed Dante by the throat and slammed him into the wall. Dante gasped and gagged, punching at Brian's arm to loosen the grip, but there was no point.

"You are a hard headed little boy," Brian snarled, "but I'm telling you, a hard head breaks easily." He gave one more squeeze and then shoved Dante to the ground and released his grip from his neck. Dante hit the ground coughing violently.

Castel looked on from the corner, staring in fear. Her body went numb with her eyes fixated on Dante. Brian walked towards her and raised his long arm, palm open. Castel looked up at Brian's arm in the air and held her breath, frozen with shock. Brian's arm came down with strength, smacking Castel in the face. Her five foot four frame dropped to the ground.

Dante managed to get himself to his feet. Leaning on the wall, he looked at his father in pure astonishment. Still coughing, he stretched out his arm toward Castel, who was lying on the ground crying. "What's wrong with you? Why'd you hit her?"

Brian couldn't care less about what his son was saying to him. He continued to stand over Castel, who slowly turned her head upward to look at Brian. She held her face as tears glistened off her cheeks.

"If I ever catch you in my home again, Mirah and John are going to lose their precious, prissy, spoiled brat. Now get OUT OF MY HOUSE!"

Castel flinched at the man's screams and glanced over at Dante, who was still leaning on the wall. Removing himself from over Castel, Brian walked to the door, only stopping to look at Dante who was too ashamed and afraid to stare his father in the face. Brian cut his eyes and left the room.

Dante exhaled and slid back to the ground, placing his hands over his face.

Castel picked herself off the floor as she wiped the tears from her face. She looked at Dante sitting on the floor. "I thought he was suppose to be gone *all* day?" she said, through her sniffles. "I guess you'll say anything to get *chicks* in your bed."

"Cut it out!" Dante finally spoke. "I thought he was going to be gone. That's what his movements have been for the last couple of weeks. So yes, that's what I told you," he finished and picked himself up off the ground.

Castel shook her head and turned her back toward him. She aggressively wiped away her tears as she picked her shirt up from the floor. Dante walked toward her and put his hand on her shoulder. He tried to speak, but Castel cut him off.

"Dante don't bother," her voice cracked. "I love you, but this is too much. First, I find out you're cheating on me, with only Lord knows how many other 'chicks' and then I get slapped by your father! The same father I told you I didn't want to run into. Seriously!"

Dante hung his head low.

"It's bad enough he beats on you, but to hit me?" she finished.

"He's not beating me," Dante defended. "I'm so sick of people and their judgments. It's tough love. I did something wrong. WE did something wrong. When you mess up there are consequences."

Castel looked at Dante in disbelief. She pushed past him, leaving the room to retrieve her shoes from the stairs. Dante waited before following behind her. He stood at the top of the steps and watched as she sat to put on her shoes, staying silent as he tried to think of something — anything to say to Castel. She finished buckling her sandals and turned to look at Dante.

"Look Cas, I apologize. I know everything with Pops has been hard on you, but he doesn't mean anything by it. I promise." He stepped down to get closer to her. "I love you Cas and…." He stopped as Brian popped up at the end of the stairs.

"I said get out of my house! NOW!!" Brian shouted.

Castel looked back at Dante, but he had his eyes on his father, staring at him with fury. She turned back towards Brian, walked down the stairs, and left the house. She went around to the back where her car was parked and proceeded to drive home, as warm tears ran down her face. She licked one away as it hit her lips. The salty taste caused to her scrunch her face and the expression revealed the pain from where Brian had hit her. She ran her hand gently across the spot, but the slightest touch caused a sharp pain to shoot down to her neck. She shook her head to get rid of the physical and emotional pain. Her feelings were beyond hurt. She felt like such an idiot. She was taken aback by Brian's actions and in disbelief about Dante. He couldn't actually be cheating on her. Could he?

"No! He's not. Brian's just tried to get under my skin like he always does with his petty remarks! I am the love of Dante's life and he is the love of mine!" Castel shouted, gripping harder on the steering wheel. "After everything we have been through? I mean we are going to have a baby!" Castel's words snapped her back to reality. She'd forgotten what a simple at-home pregnancy test had confirmed that morning. She quickly simmered down as she wondered if Brian's hit had affected her unborn child. She sucked her teeth and let out a sigh of frustration.

Pulling into her driveway, Castel rushed to get out of her car. She walked into her house and straight to the living room, not bothering to call out to her parents to see if they were home. She knew they wouldn't be as they were such workaholics. She grabbed the phone off the stand and plopped on the couch. So stressed out, she knew she had to call her best friend, Cherry. Their conversations always lifted her spirit. Castel stretched her legs as the phone dialed. Cherry's answering machine picked up and Castel just left a message. "Hey girl, it's me. When you get this message, I need you to make your way to my house ASAP. I'm ready to lose my mind." Castel hung up and threw the phone to the other sofa.

It was midnight by the time Cherry called Castel back. She promised to be over as soon as possible. Castel left the back door unlocked so Cherry could let herself in and then made her way to the freezer to retrieve one of her father's steaks. Her face had begun to swell and she put the frozen meat on her cheek to reduce the inflammation as she made her way to her bedroom to lie down.

Forty minutes later, Cherry finally arrived. She pulled into the driveway and got out the car with her dress hanging off of her. Cherry was a big party girl, who lived for the fast life. She was especially known for parading around town with older men, using them for money and other luxuries.

Tonight's behavior was no different as Cherry barely made it through Castel's back door. She staggered up the stairs, falling into the walls as she tried to keep her balance. Castel heard the commotion, got out of bed, and walked to the top of the stairs where she saw Cherry coming up, looking like a broken Raggedy Ann doll. Castel shook her head.

"Girl what is the matter with you and why do you have to make so much noise?" Castel asked crossing her arms.

Cherry let out a little chuckle as she gained her balance. "That party was so mu…" Cherry stopped in the middle of her sentence as she caught notice of Castel's face. The left side was swollen with a purple and blue bruise under her eye. Stumbling toward her, Cherry gently placed her hand on Castel's shoulder? "What happened to you face?" Cherry asked in a soft tone.

Castel stared at the ground with shame. She didn't answer.

"Did Dante hit you? Did you tell your father?" Cherry questioned with assertion. "You know he doesn't play those games!" Her voice got louder. "He will have Dante in jail ASAP! Right after he has him beat up!!"

Castel rolled her eyes as she turned around to go back into her room. Cherry was right behind her. Castel leaned against her dresser and let out a big exhale. "Dante didn't hit me Cher, his father did, and he tried to choke the life out of Dante! I'm convinced he is going crazy." Castel shook her head. "He even had the nerve to tell me, I can't come back to his house anymore!" Castel finished.

Cherry sat down on the bed in disbelief. She was no fool, she'd heard of how insane Brian was. There was always plenty of talk around town. In school there were always stories of how he beat Dante viciously as a child, but to see a glimpse of proof on Castel's face gave her chills.

Castel sat down by a disturbed Cherry, hoping she would hear some good advice. Cherry turned and looked Castel in the face.

"You have to tell your father." Cherry finally told her.

"But —"

"No buts Castel! Once you tell your father, everything will be solved and that bastard of a man, Brian, will get what he deserves! I can't believe Dante! He knows his father's ways he should have done more to make sure you were properly protected!" She lied back on Castel's bed, her rant seemingly over.

"Don't blame Dante, Cherry. It's not his fault! I don't want to be mad at him. Brian puts a lot of pressure on him and it's really unfair. Sometimes he doesn't even know what to do. If I have Brian arrested it would be too much for Dante to handle." Castel let out a sigh. "It's just more complicated than you know. I mean, for six years I have loved him and for three years now we have been going strong! We are in love," Castel confessed. "We are preparing a whole future together. We are going to graduate together… and… I mean… we are even going to have a baby together!" she revealed.

Cherry's ears rang and her blue eyes widened!! She slowly got up from the bed as she stared at her best friend in shock. "You're pregnant?" The disgust in her voice was obvious.

Castel looked at her confused. Of all the people, she thought Cherry would be happy for her. "What's the matter with you? You're supposed to be screaming for joy right now," Castel said, annoyed.

"Joy? Are you stupid? Why on earth would I be happy for you?" Cherry responded in an agitated tone!

"Because you're my best friend and you are supposed to support me!" Castel got louder.

"Why would I support you having a baby? Are you going crazy?" Cherry stood up. "Castel you have everything going for you. You are suppose to graduate early, and you're the prettiest girl in school! You can have anybody and do anything and yet you are going to be stupid enough and attach yourself to this one guy, freaking Dante Johansen, for the rest of your life? I mean come — "

"STOP CHERRY! JUST STOP! SHUT UP!" Castel hollered. "Who are you to judge me? You? A teenage, drug using, let anything and anyone between your legs whore! If anyone was suppose to judge and criticize me, I was not expecting it to be you Cherry!" Castel snapped, her heart racing with rage, as she looked Cherry in the eyes.

Cherry swallowed hard. She felt Castel's words rip through her ego. She flipped her hair, adjusted her dress, and turned around to walk out of Castel's room. Castel stood up to follow her, but Cherry stopped in the doorway and turned around to face her. "I may be all of those things Ms. Superstar, but at least I don't have a cheating boyfriend whose father hits him and me, parents who are never around and yet restrict me to their big lonely house, and most importantly, I do not have a baby growing in my stomach who is going to ruin my life." Cherry finished her sentence with a smirk.

Castel moved closer to Cherry, getting in her face so that they were eye to eye. She placed her hands on her hips and in a low tone responded, "My child will not ruin my life like your parents say you ruined theirs, but I don't blame them. And for your information, I am going to give my child everything I haven't had and more! Now get out of my big lonely house!" Castel gestured toward the stairs.

"Gladly!" Cherry waved her hand at Cherry and walked to the door. As she twisted the knob she stopped and looked back at Castel. "Can't wait to see your Maury episode, because if you think Dante is claiming that," she said, pointed at Castel's abdomen, "you're really not as smart as everyone thinks." Cherry gave Castel a big smile and then slammed the door behind her, leaving Castel standing on her steps.

Brian sat at the bar drinking a glass of scotch on the rocks. His thoughts were kicking the inside of his head and he desperately wanted the alcohol to protect him. The sight of him drilling his son into the wall was scraping away at his memory. Brian loved Dante with all his heart. Being a single dad was the greatest thing Brian had ever done in his life. Anything Dante wanted he would give him without question, but he never gained patience for Dante's hard headedness. He knew nothing else, but to teach his own son in the same way his father and brothers had taught him

Brian was the youngest of five boys and his older brother's had often beaten on him and played very aggressively. At times, Brian was left with bruises, scratches, and one time a broken arm. Any time Brian would cry they would tell him to toughen up. Brian grew up with a lot of hate in his heart for all of them. The only calmness came from his own father, who explained that his brothers were showing him love and teaching him how to survive. Brian lived with his father's words forever and ironically he saw the truth in them, as he got older. All the hits he took from his brother's made him fearless in the streets of Atlanta. He never lost a fair fight and it gained him the respect of the local drug dealers and thugs, even though he still struggled with the pain of his brother's actions. Brian definitely understood the importance of tough love and he was hoping to teach that importance to Dante. The only issue, however, was that whenever he got too physical with his son, the unhappy memories of his own childhood crept back in on him.

Brian gulped down the last of his drink to drown out the rest of his thoughts. He sat in silence a bit longer before calling Dante downstairs. "Dante I know you heard me!" Brian yelled after not getting a response.

Dante stomped downstairs, with every step getting heavier as he got downstairs. "Yeah? What's up?" Dante asked, trying to act nonchalant.

Brian cut his eyes and tried his best to ignore Dante's attitude. "Did you finish cleaning up that room?" Brian asked.

Dante rolled his eyes. "You mean, did I clean up that mess you created? Yeah, I did."

Brian cut his eyes and took a deep breath. "Don't get smart with me. I'm not in the mood."

Dante scrunched his face and sucked his teeth. Brian became more agitated at his son's disrespect and moved closer. Dante braced himself, his whole body tensing up as his father stood toe to toe with him. They looked each other in the eyes as the testosterone between them bled through the living area.

"So this is what you want to do right now? Be Mr. Tough Guy?" Brian asked in a whisper.

"Why not? I'm just as tough as you…Brian." Dante confidently responded.

A rush of fire covered Brian and with a quick motion he pushed Dante into the wall. Dante stumbled back, tripping over the center table and hit the ground with a resounding thud.

"You think so? You see that's the problem with you kids today. You think you're tougher than tough. You still have

Similac on your tongue, but you believe you're as tough as me? You're living in my house, spending my money, but you're as tough as me? Huh?" Brian antagonized, as he circled Dante's body on the ground.

Dante groaned in agony as he picked himself up. He stretched his body out as he stood straight, breathing heavily. The pain in his back made his legs weak, but his pride wouldn't let him back down. Brian had stopped circling and Dante looked at him sternly.

"That's all you care about right? Your money, and your cars, and your house? If you think I'm going to let you disrespect me *or* my girl for that, than I'm not the only one who needs to tread softly." Dante snapped at his father.

"Boy if you're not careful, I am going to hurt you in a way that'll really have everyone calling me crazy!" Brian warned taking a step closer.

"Take your best shot," Dante challenged.

In one swift movement Brian punched Dante across his face, but this time Dante fought back even though he knew he was no match for his father. The two went back and forth with blows. Dante threw the hardest punches he could, trying to hold his own against his father, but Brian wasn't phased. Brian threw body shot after body shot until he had his son against the wall. Dante desperately tried to cover his head for protection, but once defenseless, Brian grabbed Dante by the back of his neck and slammed him to the ground. Dante felt all his bones crush together as he let out a shriek of pain. Brian straightened up, breathing heavily as he stared at Dante on the ground. There was a slight smirk on his face, as if the sight of his son in pain gave him some pleasure. Dante clutched his side, moaning, which only gave Brian the urge to kick him one last time. Just as he raised his foot to squish Dante like a bug, he saw the tears glistening off his son's cheeks and a feeling of shame came over him. The urge to do any more damage dissipated and Brian no longer saw a bug, but the little boy he once was when his own brothers would throw him around. This feeling always came over Brian after Dante and him got into a fight. Brian wanted to teach his son about tough love, but he hated feeling like he was on the same level as his brothers that he had grown to hate so much. The last thing he wanted was for Dante to hate him.

Brian took a deep breath and kneeled down to help Dante off the ground. He picked him up like a baby and put Dante on the lounge chair near the bar. His father's strength was intimidating. Dante tensed up even more from fear and panic. Brian noticed Dante's uneasiness and felt even worse. Dante stretched his legs a bit to ease the pain going through his body. He glanced suspiciously at his dad who sat with his head in his hands. The two sat silently, neither one knowing where to start. Dante sat with an attitude. His pride anxiously awaited his dad to beg for his forgiveness after realizing he'd overreacted. "Everything I do for you, I do so you can have the best and be the best," Brian finally spoke through his hands. "The last thing I want is for you to stupidly jeopardize your life over these little teen flings." Brian picked his head up and directed his eyes straight toward Dante.

Dante looked at his father and thought about his words. It wasn't anything his father hadn't told him before, but this time time could sense the urgency in his dad's voice. He looked down and searched his mind for understanding, but his teenage ego came forth.

"Whatever man. I know what I'm doing. I've been good so far, right?" Dante expressed.

Brian sat up. He became annoyed at his son's immaturity. "You can say 'whatever' all you want to, but I am not going to tell you again to not bring any of those girls into my home!!" Brian asserted.

"Dad… why are you tripping so hard? I am young and the girls love me! What am I supposed to do?" Dante challenged.

"Not focus on having sex with these little girls, especially in my house!" Brian shouted. "You think it's a game, but the way you're going you're bound to get caught in a trap! I mean get serious D! What don't you understand that you're a fly young boy, athletic, and you have money! These young gold digging little girls think you're their ticket to the good life! Next thing you know they're going to drag you on Maury, claiming you are their baby's father and taking you to court for child support!" Brian's voice was assertive as he stood up in front of his son. Your future is bright and your dreams are so close to becoming a reality. I just don't want you to get caught in the nonsense!" And with that Brian walked off, not sparing his son a second glance.

Dante let out a long sigh and then slowly got up and made his way back upstairs to his room. After closing the door, he noticed Castel's shirt on the floor. He picked it up and layed down on his bed. He looked at her shirt in his hand. It was a baby pink Gucci tank. He shook his head as his father's words replayed in his head. He didn't agree. He knew that he was being careful and he trusted Castel to take care of herself. To him, his father's words didn't mean anything.

BEST FRIENDS & BOYFRIENDS

Cherry pulled into her driveway so fast her tires nearly flew off. She was flaming. Castel's words cut deep. Cherry hated reminders that her parents didn't want her, especially since they left her to live with her grandmother when she was a baby.

Cherry's mother was a Puerto Rican and Black, free spirited, fireball, and her father was a wealthy Caucasian accountant. They met in Florida at Hooters where her mother had worked. Both of her parents loved the fast life. Cherry knew that's where she got it from. They had never intended on having children, however, when her mom got pregnant with Cherry that plan went completely out the window. Cherry's parents despised her, especially her mother. Her father did not care. He didn't have to carry her for nine months and his body didn't have to go through any changes. It was the money he was spending on a baby — a baby that he didn't even want — that upset him so much.

Cherry was three months old when her parents moved to Atlanta, where Cherry's grandmother lived. They bought a nice house for the two of them to settle into and left their daughter to live with her grandmother. Dina Christopher was a seventy-two year old woman who owned a soul food diner in the town's center. She had nine children, Cherry's mother was the fifth and has always been the rebel! The stress she caused her mother was so intense that Dina suffered from a stroke at the age of sixty, which had left her with a limp.

Cherry looked up to her grandmother and was always very helpful around the house. However, Cherry's aunts and uncles came over frequently and were upset at the fact their mother was left to raise Cherry. They reminded Cherry every chance they got of her no good mother and how much she didn't want Cherry. The love her grandmother showed her was never strong enough to replace the pain her other relatives caused.

At age fourteen, Cherry began attending a high-end high school on the other side of town. This is where she met and befriended Castel. At this same time, Cherry also left her grandmother's house and started living place to place with the men she was sleeping with for money. She obtained a fake ID and started bartending in clubs. It was never hard for Cherry to fool people about her age. She looked more like twenty-three than seventeen. It probably helped that she was five foot nine, with her mother's beautiful body and her father's features of light skin, blue eyes, and light brown hair.

Cherry let out a frustrated grunt and aggressively wiped away her tears, she hated when she thought about her painful past. She got out of her car and went inside. Cherry lived in a condo just outside of Atlanta that was owned by one of sugar daddies. She met him last year when he was in Georgia on a business trip and he was more than old enough to be her father. He lived in California with his wife and children, but when he met Cherry he fell in love with everything she was. He agreed to let Cherry stay in his Georgia property after she got arrested for squatting in her last home. Cherry's only duty was to pay a small amount of rent so his wife wasn't suspicious and of course do what made him happy when he was in town.

Cherry walked in her living room and plopped on her couch. She let out a long exhale. Her thoughts ran rampant in her mind and she smirked and let out a snicker as an idea started to take shape. She sat up and reached for her purse to pull out her phone and made a call. The phone rang three times before a guy answered in a low voice on the other end.

"Hello?" a guy asked annoyed.

"Hey baby. Can you come over? I need some company. My day was a little stressful."

The guy cleared his throat. "I'm kind of tired, my day was a bit stressful as well."

Cherry sucked her teeth and leaned back on her couch. "What if I say please?" she teased playfully. "If you're stressed and I'm stressed, then we can relieve that stress together!" she giggled.

He let out a chuckle. "Alright sweetie. I can make it there in an hour, OK?"

Cherry blew a kiss through the phone. "Ok!"

She hung up the phone and ran upstairs to her room and into the walk in closet. She rummaged through her mounds of clothes and snatched up her brand new lingerie piece from Victoria's Secret. She laid it on her bed, got undressed, and jumped in the shower. The steam filled the bathroom as she let the soap lather cover her entire body. She made sure to scrub off the blood on her arms made by the needles earlier in the evening.

The hot water pierced her skin, and she stood under the spray until she was a dull red. Turning off the water, she rung the extra moisture out of her hair before drying herself off with her towel. The ceiling dripped and the walls glistened from the heat. She went into her room and slipped on the lingerie, checking her reflection in the mirror before adjusting the piece over her curvy figure.

Tucked into the mirror's edge was a picture of Castel and her. Cherry moved closer to the mirror, staring at the picture and her body became hot with anger. Just looking at Castel's face brought on feelings of annoyance and disgust. She thought of how good a friend she'd always been to Castel and all the great advice she always given her, especially when it came to her relationship with Dante. She never told her anything out of jealousy, or spite, and always respected their space. Now, Cherry could care less about Castel, her feelings, or her relationship. She could not believe Castel would disrespect her and throw her under the bus the way she did because of Dante.

Cherry softly shook her head and snatched the picture down. She took a lighter off her dresser and set the picture on fire, tossing it into the fireplace so she could watch as the flames burned black holes in Castel's pretty little face.

More than an hour passed when a car pulled up behind Cherry's silver Lincoln, the headlights shining bright through her living room windows. A tall gentleman got out the car then checked his reflection in his car mirrors. He was wearing a grey Armani suit and white striped Gucci flats. He walked up to Cherry's door and rang the bell. A few seconds later Cherry opened the door with a big smile pasted across her face. She loved seeing Dante at her door and wasn't shy as she checked him out from head to toe, appreciating his fit body. She gestured with her head for him to enter and he walked in, closing the door behind him.

He grabbed her around her waist and kissed her softly on the neck. Cherry smiled and pushed away from him. "Felt like you took a minute to get to me," she said in a low calm voice. "You didn't want to come?"

Dante chuckled as he took her hand and led her to the sofa. "Not at all," he responded. "I just have a lot on my mind and I was all over the place when you called. So, it just took me a minute to get to you that's all."

They sat down on the couch. Cherry knew exactly what he was talking about. He obviously found out about Castel being pregnant. She couldn't help but wonder what he was feeling and she desperately needed to know if he wanted to keep the baby or not.

On the couch Dante tried to get comfortable with Cherry, but she stopped him. "What's the matter? I know you're not going to let this outfit go to waste?" Dante chuckled and leaned in to kiss her.

Cherry turned her face as she removed herself from under Dante and got up from the couch. Dante let out a long sigh and sat back on the couch sucking his teeth. He didn't have time to deal with someone else's attitude, especially not some sideline. Castel was the only female whose attitude he put up with. He cleared his throat as he stared at Cherry's back. Not wanting to ignite the situation he got off the couch and walked toward her. He put his hands gently on her waist.

"What's the matter beautiful? Why you acting all funky?" Dante's voice was soft, trying to sound as genuine as possible.

Cherry removed his hands and turned around to face him. She looked into his eyes, staring as if she was trying to see into his soul, wanting to just get a glimpse into it. Dante became frustrated. He knew what that stare meant. Castel gave him that same look all the time, but he didn't like it coming from Cherry. He stepped back. "Don't do this," he told her. "What we have is good. Don't start changing on me."

Cherry sucked her teeth and pushed back with disgust. "What we have? What do we have Dante? All we do is mess around. That's nothing! We do not have anything!" Cherry explained, with hand gestures in Dante's face.

"You knew that from the start! What's your problem Cherry?" Dante was confused and not in the mood. "Is this what you called me over here for? To give me some kind of lecture? Well, no thanks. I have better things to do!" Dante turned and walked to the door.

Cherry followed behind him and just as he reached for the doorknob, she yelled out, "Oh yeah? Lectured about how to be a father?" Her words rolled off her tongue like balls of fire.

Dante's ears popped from Cherry's words. He felt his heart skip two beats. He slowly turned back around and looked at Cherry. "What? Who are you talking about?" His tone was low as he moved toward her. His tall, built frame, toppling over her.

Cherry rolled her eyes and crossed her arms. She turned her head, trying to not appear intimidated. "You heard me! Don't play like you don't know your perfect little wife is pregnant with your perfect little baby. The two of you can just be the perfect little family." Cherry's words were filled with sinful envy.

Dante stumbled back and sat on the arm of the couch in disbelief. Tears began to well in his eyes. His demeanor took Cherry by surprise. She quickly realized that Castel hadn't told him yet. A beautiful opportunity racked her mind. She moved toward him to show him comfort. To her it was finally a chance to pull Dante away from Castel for good.

Cherry leaned her body against Dante's and gave him a hug. He pressed his face against her chest and cried softly. "It can't be. That's not true. Castel always said she didn't want to be a mother before her time. She always made sure she was the one watching out for a pregnancy." His words were muffled as he sobbed, his tears wetting Cherry's skin.

She rubbed his back as he lifted his head from her chest. He let out a long loud exhale and got up from the arm of the couch, walking toward the door. Cherry followed behind him.

"It's okay babe. I would be upset too if my girlfriend was having a baby by another guy." Cherry's lies rolled off of her tongue like a sweet serenade. "Just get your DNA tested and then you won't have to deal with her irresponsible behavior," she continued.

Dante turned around in confusion. "Excuse me? What are you talking about? Castel is the one pregnant right? We're talking about the same girl, aren't we?"

"Of course we are," Cherry expressed with certainty and put her arms to her sides.

"Then why are you mentioning a DNA test? Castel's baby is all mine. She's not like that," Dante assured Cherry, as he stepped back.

Cherry put her hands on her hips and gave Dante a stern look. "Dante you're not serious? Even I thought you would be smarter than that. You never underestimate your opponent." Cherry imitated the voice of Madea and gave a slick smile.

Dante was beyond shocked. He knew he did what he wanted behind Castel's back, but he always believed she was a good girl and a loyal girlfriend. They would always have conversations about other girls in their school, who would sleep with multiple guys. In the eyes of Castel, they were whores and she prided herself in never being like them.

Dante could not believe it. His stomach knotted, as the feeling of heartbreak ravished his body. Cherry went to reach for him, but he pushed her away and stormed out the door. Cherry stood in her living room, unsatisfied. She thought her actions would cause Dante to say it was over with Castel, but instead he defended her, and she was left all alone and feeling like an idiot. She hated the feeling. Tears began to well up in her eyes, but she took a deep breath and brushed them off.

Wanting and needing her current emotions numb, Cherry ran upstairs to her bedroom and went into her closet. She pulled out her black toolbox with her best friends in it. She did three lines first, then four more. After her last line, Cherry laid back on her bed and let her mind wander as she drifted into her happy place.

Dante sped back home with fury. He couldn't believe what Cherry had told him. Castel of all people, cheating on him? And to add salt to a wound she was pregnant, with a baby that was not his? Tears of anger ran down his face. He gripped so hard on the steering wheel, it was as if he wanted to rip it out of the car. He pulled into his driveway, almost driving through the garage. He got out of his car, slamming the door and went into the house where he began to pace back and forth, his thoughts meandering all over the place. His brain felt like it was going to melt and ooze out of his ears. He started punching and kicking the walls until sweat dripped down his face and his heart thumped so hard he could feel it coming out of his chest. He punched, and punched, and punched the walls, until the skin on his knuckles peeled off and blood dripped to the ground.

Once Dante finally calmed down, he went upstairs to his bathroom and ran the water to wash his hands. He let the smoky hot water run over his knuckles to wash away the dark red blood that had begun to dry. As he turned off the faucet and looked in the mirror, he saw the burning pain in his eyes and felt the hate building for a girl he once had the most love for. Considering all of the women Dante slept with on the side, he'd always made sure to never knock up anyone because he didn't want to hurt Castel in such a way. He couldn't believe she would be so selfish and careless. It seemed impossible that she would chose to hurt him this much. Dante let out a sigh filled with disbelief, and then wiped his hands on the nearby towel, before retiring to his bed for the night.

TREMBLING CASTLE

Castel stood in her bathroom, looking in the mirror at her growing baby bump. She tried to suck it in, but that only caused a sharp pain to shoot through her body. She hadn't heard from Cherry in two weeks and she missed her ride, or die, pale girl. Cherry hadn't returned any of her calls or messages and deep down Castel was worried. She even considered asking her Dad to look into it, but she didn't want to create a situation. Knowing Cherry, she was probably relaxing at some guy's house and would turn up eventually. The thought made her think of Dante. She had spoken to him on the phone a couple of days ago, but she had yet to tell him about the pregnancy. She didn't feel it was the right time, especially since her parents were busy getting together her big birthday party. The event was still a few days off, but they had been planning it for years.

"Castel!" Her mother Mirah yelled from downstairs, breaking her from her trance.

"Yeah, Mom. What is it?"

"Come downstairs, I want to talk to you."

Uh oh, Castel instantly thought. Usually, when her mother wanted to talk to her about something she just came to her room. What could she possibly want? Castel walked downstairs and went into the living room. Her mother was standing in the doorway of the front door. She flashed Castel a smile and gestured her hand for Castel to come outside.

"Come on. Come take a look," Mirah said, as a beaming smile came across her face. Castel walked faster to get outside and when she walked onto the front porch she was amazed to see a white, two door, BMW, sitting in the driveway. Her father, John, stood next to it, his left arm extended, jingling the keys in this hand.

"Happy Birthday, baby girl!! It is all yours, and of course you deserve it!" John explained, stretching out both arms.

Castel ran to her father and hugged him tightly as if she wanted to puncture every organ in his body. "Thank you! Thank you! Thank you Daddy! I love you so much! " Castel expressed.

"Hey! I had a hand in this too. Can I get some love?" Mirah asked from behind.

Castel wrapped her arms around both of her parents with tears of joy forming in her eyes.

"Oh sweetie, you deserve it. As long as you continue to keep those beautiful grades, and be our wonderful responsible princess, we will give you the world," John explained.

Her father's words made Castel's ears ring. How could she tell them she was pregnant now? She would be delivering the biggest disappointment of their lives. She lifted her head from her father's shoulder, took the keys from his hand, and walked back into the house. Her parents looked at each other puzzled. In her bedroom, Castel plopped on her bed and the tears that fell tore holes in the pillowcase. She felt like a failure. She started to think that Cherry was right; she was in over her head. She needed to talk to Dante and get his opinion on everything. It was the only way she would feel better.

The day of Castel's party finally arrived. It was at one of Brian's clubs and she pleaded with her parents to change the location, but they weren't having it, so she refused to leave her room.

"I don't understand Cas. When we started planning you were so excited. You can't just not go!" her mother explained.

"I don't care! I don't want to have this party and that's that! So please leave me alone!"

John let out a long sigh and left the room. Mirah sat next to her daughter. Her mother's intuition shot through her spirit.

"Castel is everything okay with you and Dante?" she questioned.

Castel hated her mother's intuition. She gave her mother a side-eye and quickly turned her head, but the tears came rushing down her face. "Mother please, I don't want to go, so let's drop it," her voice cracked.

"I think you've lost your mind. I didn't raise some weak girl. You are so much better than that boy or some high school relationship. Cut the crying," Mirah scolded.

Wiping her tears, Castel turned back to her mother. "Mother, just leave it alone, okay? It's not that easy to explain or even let go. You won't understand, so please leave it alone."

Mirah reached for her daughter, but Castel pushed her away and left the room. She grabbed her sneakers, hoping that a walk would help settle her mind. As she opened the door she found Dante standing on the front porch.

"Happy birthday," he said nonchalantly. "I didn't get you a gift. I knew you wouldn't mind."

Castel rolled her eyes. Being the son of a business mogul, she never understood how Dante could be so cheap. She stepped down to the porch and closed the door behind her.

"Where are you going?" Dante asked, though he didn't really care.

"I'm going out. Do you mind walking with me?" Castel looked Dante in his eyes. She knew they weren't on good terms, but she still wanted to see if the love was there.

Dante gave her a slight smile, grabbed her by the hand, kissing her cheek. "Nah, I came here for you." He gave her a slight smile.

They walked to the park. Castel's thoughts were all over the place. As they sat on the benches, she began to tear up.

She wondered whether or not she should tell Dante about her pregnancy. Dante noticed the tears welling in Castel's eye. He thought to himself, "Yea, go ahead and feel bad. You should, after what you've done to me. Shameless whore!" He knew not to actually say that though. He knew to act as if he didn't know anything. Instead he put his hand gently under her chin and turned her face until their eyes met.

As they looked into each other's eyes, Castel's stomach turned. It seemed as if Dante's hazel eyes were piercing her soul. Now was the time. She shook the butterflies off, opened her mouth, and with a low cracking voice she whispered, "I'm pregnant."

Although he already knew, something about it coming from Castel's mouth made it a reality.

Castel continued to look at Dante, but caught a cold chill when he moved his hand from hers and looked at the ground. She put her arm around his shoulders, consoling him. "It's okay, Baby. I know it's a big shock, but I am a big girl. Everything will be okay." Castel ran her fingers through his long thick locks, as he let out a big sigh.

He turned to look at Castel and asked, "So have you told the father yet?"

Castel's ears rang from his words. She looked at him puzzled, and felt her body go numb. She removed her arm from around Dante and leaned back with a serious look. "You're joking, right? You don't mean that." Castel still looked at Dante, trying to seek an answer through his eyes.

Dante sat up straight, inhaled, and then let out a long sigh. He leaned back, folding his arms and looked away. In that moment he wanted to reveal the whole truth of what he'd heard from Cherry. Castel waited for an answer, but could see that Dante wasn't joking. She couldn't believe that he thought of her like that. Her of all people? Castel looked to the ground in disgust. Her heart raced, her blood boiled, and a knot formed in her throat. With one swift motion she backhanded Dante, busting open his bottom lip.

Dante jumped up in shock. He touched his lip, looking as his fingers, which were ruby red with blood. He looked down at Castel, who had fire in her eyes. He chuckled and wiped the blood off with his shirt. Castel did not move. She wasn't afraid. Her father had taught her well when it came to self-defense, but Dante simply stretched his arms out to the side and dusted himself off. He flared his nose, looking Castel up and down. "Like I said, go find your baby father. Once you drop that load and get that body back, then, come and holla at me. You know you came in handy when I needed to break in a box spring." Dante's words sent a sharp pain through Castel's body. She dropped back down on the bench and sat frozen, her heart heavy, her stomach in knots. Tears fell from her eyes as she watched Dante walk away. She folded her arms around her body, sat back, and cried in the middle of the park.

Dante hurried home. He needed to tell his dad what happened. He walked through the front door with sweat dripping from his face. His white polo shirt was drenched and clung to his body. He slammed the door behind him and walked into the living room, plopping down on the couch. He laid there as thoughts ran rampant through his mind. He really did love Castel. He used to think about their future; their life after school, marriage, and yes, children, but he refused to take care of another guy's baby. He knew he did his dirt, but to him Castel was always supposed to be there with him. His number one and her only.

He sat up on the couch. He felt his body getting hot with anger all over again. He balled up his fists and closed his eyes tightly. Tears began to fall. He kicked the center table and shuttered as it slammed on the floor. Picture frames crashed with a loud bang. Brian, who was sitting in the foyer, hurried into the living room. He observed the shattered glass on the floor, and his son, tense and angry, on their couch. Folding his arms, he leaned on the wall and asked, "Did you lose your mind? Is the money to pay for all of this coming out of your pocket?"

Dante lightly shook his head and let out a little chuckle. He turned to look at his father, pain still in his eyes. "Can you at least ask me what's wrong, first? Or is your money more important?" Dante's voice cracked a bit as he finished his sentence. He hated that his father was always more concerned about his stuff than his son.

Brian snickered, walked to the table, and picked it up. He looked at Dante and said, "I hadn't realized that your mother had signed over her rights for me to raise an emotional female, who can never take a joke."

Dante's bottom lip rolled up in disbelief. He opened his mouth to say something, but his father burst into laughter.

"Chill, I'm joking." He threw his hands up. "I'm joking, son. I haven't seen you cry in years. What's gotten into you?"

Dante looked at him oddly. It seemed like Brian was being sincere, and for once, he said the right thing to him at the right time. Dante sighed. "Castel's pregnant."

There was an awkward silence. Brian leaned back on the couch. "Is that all?"

Dante's eyebrows rose.

"Is that all?" he repeated.

"After all of the lectures you've been giving me? That's all you're going to say? I thought you'd be pissed?" Dante said.

"Boy, please," Brian started, as he got up and walked to the bar. "After all of the lectures, you still didn't listen. I knew you'd knock somebody up. I just didn't think it would be that girlfriend of yours."

"It's not mine!" Dante stated. "That's why I'm so upset."

Brian turned around with a shocked look on his face. "Wow. Ha ha," he laughed. "I didn't think the perfect princess had it in her." Brian chuckled again as he poured himself a glass.

Dante looked down at the floor. His father was mocking him and he hated it.

"So who's the father?" Brian sipped his drink.

"I don't know," Dante looked at him. "She didn't tell me."

"Well," Brian shook his head, "I guess she thought it didn't matter. At least she told you it wasn't yours."

"Actually, she didn't tell me. Her best friend, Cherry told me."

"Wait. What?" Brian placed the cup on the bar top. "You accused her based off of something someone told you?"

"It wasn't just anybody, Dad. It was her best friend. Cherry is the one person who knows her better than me. They spend the majority of their time together, sharing secrets, and whatnot."

"Hold on. Didn't you sleep with Cherry, too? Now you're really going to be on Maury." His father laughed again.

"Yea, so what?"

"So what?" Brian stared at him. "No matter what a woman says, if you chill with them, they catch feelings. They are emotional creatures and every woman wants someone to call their own." Brian finished his drink.

Regardless of what his father said, Dante still believed Cherry was telling the truth. He left his father and went upstairs to his room. He plopped down on the bed and sighed. He wanted to clear his mind because he wasn't one to be stressed. He decided to call his best friend, Josh, so they could hit up the club.

"Hey," he said into the phone when Josh answered. "You tryna go out? I need to loosen up."

QUICKLY SLIPPING

"You have to give me something!" Cherry yelled through the phone. "Stop acting like that! I never let you down!" Cherry's hair was frazzled and her body was sweating and shaking. She'd relapsed after being clean for a year and half with Castel's help. Castel had gotten Cherry to give up drugs when she decided she wanted to be a part of the cheer team, but now with the loss of her support, Cherry was no longer strong enough to resist. Her body was going through withdrawal and she desperately needed a fix from her D-boy.

"I'm not buying what you're selling Cherry! I want my money!" His deep scratchy voice choked Cherry's eardrums. "Every time you call me, I have to listen to another excuse from your broke behind and I am done," the voice shouted and hung up.

Cherry was quiet as the dial tone buzzed in her ear. She sat numb for a long moment, biting her lip so hard that she almost chewed it off, and then suddenly she jumped up and began rummaging through her house, looking through the closets and all of the dresser draws. She was hoping to find a dollar, a nickel, a penny, something. Her heart was pounding and she stopped for a moment and took a deep breath.

"Okay, Okay. I know I have money somewhere. I have to… Oh, I know. I…I'll call Josh. Yeah, I will call Josh and he will give me some money," she said out loud. Cherry ran down the hall and grabbed her phone. She quickly dialed Josh's number. She could always count on him to be there when she needed something. They use to date, but Cherry thought Josh was controlling. She was a free spirit who liked to come and go as she pleased, so in the end Josh got tired of trying to make a girlfriend out of Cherry. He never stopped loving her though, so they still kept in touch. Cherry enjoyed having him to call on too. With no family to count on, Josh was the greatest comfort she ever had.

She dialed his number. "Come on," she said impatiently.

"Hello," his deep voice finally answered.

"Josh? Josh, I need some money, please?" she begged. "I'm dying!"

Josh sucked his teeth. It was cool to still be Cherry's friend, but he was sick and tired of only hearing from her when she needed something. It was frustrating to feel like she only wanted to know him for all of his hard earned money.

Taking a deep breath, he replied, "I'm sorry, shorty. I don't have it right now. My money —"

"Josh," Cherry interrupted with an attitude, "I know you got some money. You just got paid," she revealed.

"And I got bills, my own expenses, and my own life to deal with! You and your frivolous expenses are no longer a concern of mine, so I don't have to answer to you. Find someone else to call and let me have my peace." Josh hung up the phone.

Cherry tossed her phone across the room in a fit of frustration. The phone hit the wall and shattered the screen. Cherry blew up, throwing everything around the room. She punched the walls and destroyed whatever her hands could touch. "I can't believe he hung up on me," Cherry said out loud in a distorted tone.

She stood in the middle of her destroyed room, her hair and clothes disheveled. Her body shook and sweat dripped off her skin. She let out a scream of anger, as she hit herself in the head and jumped up and down. She thrashed herself about, stumbling into the hallway. Her body banged against the walls as she pulled her hair. Without her best friend, her drugs, or even Josh to turn to, she was quickly losing her mind. "I hate them. I freaking hate them!" she grunted through her teeth.

So full of rage, Cherry paid no attention to the staircase at her feet. With one more step she tumbled down to the bottom floor, letting out a loud scream as she hit the ground. Her shoulder busted open and blood gushed out. Cherry groaned in agony. Tears ran down her cheeks as she lay on the floor. She tried her best to move so that she could get to the house phone, but her right leg was stuck in between the railings. In too much pain to get up and work her way out, she cried, "Lord! Please." With no help in sight, she remained on the floor as the blood pooled around her.

Castel stretched across her bed. All she wanted to do was clear her mind. She was fed up with everyone and refused to think about anyone else's nonsense. Just as she was dozing off into a deep sleep, her phone rang. It was her father, John. She sucked her teeth and hit the reject button. They hadn't been on speaking terms since she refused to go to her birthday party that had cost him thousands of dollars. She didn't know or care why he was calling. She rolled over into a comfortable position to fall back to sleep. As she drifted off once more, the phone rang again. Castel sucked her teeth and reached for it. It was her father calling again.

"Ugh," she exclaimed. She knew that he would never stop calling, so she answered. "Yea, Dad?" Her voice was groggy and irritated.

"It took you long enough, Castel. This is an emergency. What did I tell you about paying attention to your phone?" John scolded.

Castel sat up in the bed, annoyed at her father. "I missed your call once. What's the problem? What's so urgent? I am trying to sleep," she snipped.

"I need you to get to the hospital, now." he told her.

Castel jumped out of the bed. "The hospital? What? Why? Are you okay? Where's Mom?" she asked frantically. "Is it Dante?" she panicked.

"Dante? What? No." John sucked his teeth. "Just hurry up and get here."

"No, Dad. What's going on?" Being the Chief of Police, Castel naturally worried about her father every time he left the house. Various scenarios started to run through her head. Her mother was currently in the hospital due to chronic stress. Maybe something more serious was wrong with her? She'd hit Dante pretty hard the other day. Had she broken something?

"Castel, sweetie, calm down. It's not your mother or me. It's not Dante either." John assured her.

"Then, what's the emergency, Dad?"

"It's Cherry. She fell down the stairs and hurt herself really bad. One of the neighbors had to break the door down just to get to her. She's stable, but sweetie, she's lost a bit of blood and…" John stopped as he realized Castel wasn't saying anything on the other end.

"Castel?" he called.

Castel didn't answer. She was too numb. She's hadn't talked to Cherry since they'd argued. Now, her best friend was lying in a hospital. Guilt covered her.

"Castel?" John called again.

"I'll be there, Dad," Castel said. "Is she going to be okay?"

"Yes, Hun, she is."

Castel didn't believe him though. She hung up the phone and grabbed her keys.

MISGUIDED LOVE

The early afternoon sun beamed down on Dante's back. Dante peeked from under the vomit stained shirt covering his head to look at the time. The clock on the wall read one o'clock in the afternoon. He sucked his teeth and sat up. Drinking was Dante's way of numbing the pain, he was definitely Brian's son. Brian's love for alcohol was one of the reasons he'd opened his clubs, but it was always a temporary sedative to the hurt. Dante's thoughts still tore through his head. Castel was the first thought that came across his mind and he felt rage bleed through his spirit.

Shaking it off, he climbed out of bed and stumbled down the hall to the bathroom. While he brushed his teeth, he noticed scratches on his chest. He ran his fingers down each of them and sighed. "Who did I lay down with now?" he chuckled to himself. Dante quickly finished in the bathroom and went to grab a shirt before going downstairs. He didn't want his father to play investigator on his body.

Brian was burning in the kitchen as he did every morning. No longer married, he'd made sure he knew how to cook for himself and his son.

"Morning," Brian greeted. "You've been taking shots to the head, huh?" Brian asked sarcastically. "It took Joe and Red to carry you in this time," Brian revealed, as he placed the food on the plates.

Dante chuckled. Though he was underage, the bouncers and bartenders still treated him like everyone else. Of course, they were only trying to avoid the drama. None of them wanted to lose their jobs and the last thing Brian cared about was Dante's drinking habit. He believed alcohol made a man strong, the same way his father taught him.

Dante sat down at the island and looked at the food on the plate; a big t-bone steak, eggs, and potatoes with fruit on the side and then he looked up at Brian. "You turning into Friendly's?" he asked.

Brian gave Dante a smug look. "Don't hate on my skills. You need to sit in this kitchen one day and watch me throw down, instead of always coming when I'm finished. You might learn a thing or two."

"You know I'm on a strict diet. If I watched you cook *and* learned how to cook like *this*, psssh. I would be twice the size," Dante joked as he let out a laugh.

"O please boy. I've watched you play football for the last ten years and I've also fed you for the last ten years. My cooking skills won't stop you from being on your A-game," Brian insisted through bites.

Dante threw a few more bites of food into his mouth with a gulp of juice. "I hope not. This is senior year and all the scouts are going to be out there, so I gotta be in tip top shape," Dante expressed, as he gasped for air.

"Well slow down and don't kill yourself before the season starts," Brian laughed, as he watched his son stuff more and more food in his mouth. Brian let out a soft chuckle, took a few more bites of his food and then placed the rest in the microwave.

"The man of leftovers," Dante teased.

Brain gave Dante a smirk and then walked out to the den. Dante reached into his pajama pocket and pulled out his phone. There were three text messages — one from Josh and two from Castel. Dante frowned at the thought of her. He was still pissed about the baby and refused to have any concern for her. Josh's text was a reminder for the pre-season football practice that was set to happen in two weeks. It was a way for the coaches to see how well the senior players kept up since football camp. Dante wasn't worried about that though.

He finished the last bit of food on his plate, threw it in the sink, and went into the den where his father was sitting at the bar, shining his bottles of liquor. Dante shook his head as he stretched out on the couch. Just as he got comfortable the doorbell rang. Dante sucked his teeth and continued to lie on the couch. Brian looked over at Dante's motionless body.

"I wonder who that is?" he stated sarcastically.

"Can't be anyone for me, and if it is… I'm not here." Dante lay still motionless on the couch.

Brian sucked his teeth and gave Dante an awful side eye he couldn't see. He put down the tequila bottle he was shining and walked to the door. There in the doorway was Brian's ex-wife and Dante's mother, Lorena.

Brian and Lorena got married right after high school graduation. After the young couple discovered she was pregnant with their son. From the beginning, being a young wife and mother was far from the plan Lorena had envisioned for her life. When Dante was just three months old, she'd left for law school. Now, as a District Attorney, she was always too busy to spend time with her son.

Brian rolled his eyes at the sight of her as he leaned against the wall. "To what do we owe this pleasure, Madam District Attorney?" he asked sarcastically.

Lorena let out a light chuckle and let herself in. She walked into the den where Dante was still laying comfortably on the couch.

"Good morning sweetheart," she greeted Dante, as she gently placed her things on the sectional.

Dante continued to relax on the couch. Lorena paused waiting for a reply. She looked back at Brian who was still by the door. Annoyed, Lorena gestured for help. Brian rolled his eyes, shut the door and walked to the den. "Hey, D? Get up. Your *wonderful* mother is here," Brian expressed jokingly, as he gave Lorena a smile.

"Cute! I see some things never change," she replied with a smirk.

Brian paused. "Well, if you came by more often, more change would probably occur," Brian chastised.

"Do you have to do this every time I come here? Can I get one visit without your nonsense?" Lorena asked annoyed.

"You're asking a lot for a person who visits so rarely Lo-re-na!" Brian shot again.

The two bickered back and forth as Dante cringed on the couch. Seventeen years of life and not one memory of his parents having a happy conversation. Every time they were actually in the same space, they didn't do anything but throw dirt on one another. His father always started it and Dante figured it was because there was some lingering pain from when Lorena had left them and Brian had never truly gotten over it. Dante never blamed his dad though. In fact, Dante didn't need his dad to talk down about his mom. The older he got the easier it was for him to catch on that he would always be second to Lorena's career.

"Uhhhhhh boy!" Dante finally shouted, as he sat up on the couch. Brian and Lorena silenced their arguing at the sound of his voice. "Well now that you guys are done destroying my ear drums... how about we actually try and have a conversation about me this time and not your hidden love for each other." Dante gave them a joking smile.

Brian rolled his eyes at his son's attempt to play peacemaker. Lorena took a sharp inhale and then finally sat down next to Dante. His body stiffened. Silence peeled off the walls.

"So, how have you been?" Lorena asked, breaking the silence.

"Great," Dante replied dryly, staring at his hands.

"What have you been up to?" she tried again with more enthusiasm.

Dante let out a deep breath. He knew he had to engage in this conversation or Lorena would do nothing but ask more superficial questions. He sat up and cleared his throat. "Well, you know... a little bit of this, a little bit of that. Shoot, I'm so busy I'd lose my feet if I didn't need them to run." Dante chuckled, as he motioned like he was on the field.

"Oh that's right, this is your last year. You're a senior this year. Congratulations! I'm so proud of you," Lorena joyfully expressed.

Dante felt proud to see her excited. Brian looked on with a slight smile. He was surprised, yet happy to see Lorena genuinely interested in their son.

"So D, remind me," Lorena continued, "what position do you play on the basketball team?"

Brian's heart dropped. Dante gave her a look of confusion and Lorena caught a lump in her throat as she realized her error. She glanced over at Brian, whose face was written with disgrace. Lorena hung her head in shame.

"Sorry…it's football. Football. Sorry." Her words dropped hard from her lips.

A cloud of pity came over Dante. He'd seen his mother fake her interest about many things in his life, but he didn't get that feeling this time. He believed in her interest. Not knowing the sport he played was simply her absenteeism catching up with her. He took a moment and then placed his arm around her shoulder. "You're good, Ma. I get my own favorite sports mixed up most of the time," he joked.

Lorena smiled at her son's compassion. "Well, I won't be mixing up your sport anymore," she promised, as she patted him on the knee.

"Does this mean you'll show up to a game or two this season?" Brian chimed in.

Lorena shot him an annoyed look across the room. Brian stood with his arms crossed. The last thing he was doing was falling for Lorena's sorrow act. He stopped that years ago. Lorena rolled her eyes and turned her attention back to Dante.

"I would love to come to one of your games. When is it?" She asked.

"September 28th!" Dante told her cheerfully.

"Coach is pumping us up for it because most of the scouts are coming down that day. It's going to be huge." He expressed.

He jumped up from his seat and rummaged through the papers on the computer table. He snatched a flyer and sat back down.

"This is all the information for the first game and on the back are the dates for the other games." He told her.

"I'll mark them down … I promise." Lorena said eagerly. She pulled out her blackberry and put it in her calendar.

"It's locked in, so I won't forget." She uttered.

She gave him a joyous smile and then reached her arm over him and patted him on the back. Dante flinched aggressively at his mother's touch that reignited the pain from the bruise of his father slamming him on the wall. Lorena quickly removed her hand.

"Are you okay? Are you hurt?" She questioned.

"Yeah, I'm fine. It's just a little practice injury that's still messing with me. I'm good." Dante let out a nervous chuckle.

He quickly glanced over at his dad who was staring out the window, pretending to not hear the conversation. Dante looked away, desperately hoping his mother hadn't followed his eyes to Brian, but she easily made the connection. Lorena took a sharp inhale and then forced a smile.

"You better be careful. The last thing we need is an injury this season. Or at all," she told him, as she looked in Brian's direction. "How about you go upstairs and relax your back? I've taken up enough of your time today," she finished.

Dante gave her a slight smile and nodded. He made his way upstairs, keeping his head down as he passed his father. Lorena waited for Dante to be out of sight before she stood up to gather her things. She slowly walked in Brian's direction, who was still standing nonchalantly at the window.

"I see you still have your same old anger problems." Lorena started.

"Oh please, Lorena. Don't start your fake psychology crap. I'm not in the mood." Brian shut her down.

"Of course you aren't. You never are… but you will be when I send child services through this door to take him out of here," she threatened, as she moved closer.

Brian slowly turned and faced her. "How dare you? You get one good day with him and you think that gives you the right to insult and question how I raise my boy?" Brian's voice got louder.

"Abuse is not raising a child or haven't you got that through your thick skull?" Lorena challenged.

"According to the memories in my thick skull, you've never raised a child to even know the answer to that question. I wonder how all your attorney colleagues would feel about their beloved D.A. neglecting her own child?" Brian intimidated.

Lorena's palms started to sweat. She knew Brian could see the fear in her eyes. Lorena loved her career and in her line of work any amount of negative press was a complete career killer.

Brian gave her a sly look. He knew he had her by the strings…as usual. "Not so confident in your words now, are you?" he asked with a smirk.

Lorena swallowed hard. She wanted to punch him in the throat as viciously as she could.

"Instead of being so worried about calling child services on me, how about you make sure you actually show up to his game in September? Like a good little mother," Brian insulted.

The smirk on his face made Lorena's stomach knot. Her urge to hit him grew, but she knew she couldn't actually take Brian. She softly growled under her breath, adjusted her purse, and then made her way to the door. Brian stepped over to avoid being bumped. He knew how petty Lorena could be. He watched as she got to the door, but then stopped.

"I'll be at his game. You better believe I'll be there. You just make sure he gets there in one piece!" she informed and then left the house, aggressively closing the door.

Brian continued to stand in the den as Lorena's words echoed in his ears. Dante stood by his bedroom door, disturbed as well by his mother's words. Would his mother really call child services on his dad? What if they took him out the house? Would he get foster care? What would happen to his football career? A million thoughts ran through his mind. The last thing he needed this school year was a scandal. No school would dare accept a football star with deplorable home conditions. Dante let out a loud grunt and walked over to his bed. He threw the pillows to the ground and dropped down on his back. He covered his face and breathed softly to himself. All he wanted was to clear his mind. He let out another grunt and then dropped his hands on his stomach.

"Ah shoot. Dang man!" he shrieked, forgetting the scratches covering his body.

He quickly got up and went to the bathroom, taking off his shirt to examine his battle wounds. He ran his fingers down each scratch. A few had dried blood that Dante hoped was his. He continued to look in the mirror as his phone started to ring in his bedroom, but he ignored it and took some cotton balls and alcohol out of the cabinet. He cringed as the burning sensation lit his entire body. His phone began to ring again. "Oh boy," he expressed. He walked to his room to answer. It was Josh. "Yeah? What's up?" Dante asked in an irritated voice.

"About time!" Josh shouted through the phone. "What you doing?"

"I was in the bathroom. Yo, was I in a fight last night? My chest is messed up." Dante walked back to the bathroom and started the shower.

Josh chuckled. "Nah. Well, not the kind of fight you're thinking of." Josh's laugh got deeper.

Dante paused. "No. . . I didn't? Not again?" Dante questioned.

"Yeah, again Bro. You know you get reckless… and she was a pretty little thing too." Josh let out another laugh. "She wasn't as pretty as Cas though so I guess that's your plus."

"Do you hear yourself? That isn't a plus! What's wrong with you?" Dante shouted through the phone.

"D, calm down. I didn't call to argue and since we're on the topic of females, you never finished telling me what happened with Cas and why they shut down her party." Josh tried changing the subject.

"I could care less about her or that stupid party. Don't play with me Josh. What's the point of having you around me if you don't have my back in situations like this? Like who was she? Where did we do it at?" Dante asked, agitated. The whole reason he started taking Josh with him to the club was so he could stop him from having random drunken sex, but he proved on more than one occasion to be completely helpless.

"Hold on. Relax. This time was *not* my fault. I told you, last night I had to go to check on Cherry. She got hurt real bad."

Dante's annoyance grew. "You left me to check on that trick? Since when has she ever stopped what she was doing for you? Of all the people to put above me!" Dante ranted.

"Yo, Dante, chill! I didn't put anyone before you. Cherry has no one! She was busted up and the police needed someone there to help them answer questions about her," Josh explained.

Josh did his best to try and calm his friend but Dante was not trying to hear it. "You were supposed to look out for me. If the police were dealing with Cherry then I know Castel was there for her, which means you decided to leave me hanging." Dante hung up the phone. He was so frustrated. Why couldn't he ever get someone to rely on? Why was everyone always so…disloyal?

SENTIMENT

Castel slowly opened the door to Cherry's room. Her best friend was lying there with tubes running from her body and a bag of fluids hanging over her. The sight made Castel cringe. She couldn't remember Cherry ever having so much as a cold. She was always the life of the party, especially when she was drunk.

Castel sat down in a chair next to the bed. She stared at Cherry in disbelief, a knot formed in her throat, as her tongue went numb, and her stomach began to hurt. Seeing Cherry like this was giving her a new sense of pain and she couldn't hold back her tears.

"Why? Why is all of this happening?" she cried out softly. She sniffled and leaned back in the chair and then stomped her foot on the ground in frustration, which caused a sharp pain to shoot through her stomach. For a minute she had forgotten that she was pregnant. Obviously, all of this was not helping the baby. She wiped her tears as she rubbed her lower stomach. Castel leaned back in the chair, closed her eyes, and stretched out her legs, trying to relax her mind and not think about anything.

"Castel?" she heard a voice call. "Castel?" the voice called again.

Castel opened her eyes to see her father standing over her. She gave him a smile and fixed herself in the chair. He patted her head and stepped aside. A doctor was checking on Cherry. A nurse stood by the door, taking notes. They examined Cherry, moving from one side of the bed to the other. They pulled down her gown at the shoulder, revealing a rather large wound, covered by gauze. Castel laid her head on her father's shoulder and wept. He hugged her as tears stained his uniform.

"Please! Her wounds are not extensive," the doctor assured. "She's pretty banged up. Multiple bruises and a concussion, but she should heal nicely in a few weeks. However, we found something in her blood work," the doctor continued.

Castel sat up. The doctor flipped his paper and walked over to John and Castel. She started to think the worst. Cherry probably had cancer, or severe head trauma, or kidney disease from all of her notorious partying. "What's wrong with her?" Castel finally asked.

The doctor paused. "We found heroine in her blood."

"What?" John jumped up. "Heroine?" he questioned with undisguised disgust. He knew Cherry was a troubled young lady, but he never thought she would go any further than alcohol. He turned to Castel. "Did you know she was using drugs?" John asked.

"No. I…" Castel stammered.

"Don't you dare lie to me young lady? You are around her more than anyone else and you're telling me you didn't know she was on drugs?" John's voice cracked the walls.

"Dad please, I didn't know she went back to the drugs," she explained.

"Back on drugs?" John became more infuriated.

"Yes, Dad. Please, listen. When I met her… when she first came to school, she was addicted, but coach and I got her to quit when she joined the team. I thought she was clean for good. I thought it was just the alcohol. I only knew about her drinking." Castel's voice cracked as she held onto her father's hand. She had no idea Cherry was back on drugs and now she was pissed at her for putting her at the front end of her nonsense.

John looked at her with a long pause, testing his daughter's words.

"Please, I didn't mean to cause any trouble, but I did have to inform you." the doctor explained, breaking the eye contact between father and daughter. "We notified the police who accompanied the EMS who brought her here. They told us to hold her. She will be read her rights as soon as she is conscious enough to understand.

"Wait a minute!" Castel jumped up out of her seat. "How can you just arrest a teenager?"

"According to the identification the EMS found in her house, she is eighteen."

Castel bit her lip as her father said, "I guess you didn't know about the fake ID either?" His sarcasm burned. John rolled his eyes and then gave his full attention to the doctor.

"Please, doctor I am Chief John Rogers. Can you please tell me which of the officers you spoke to?" John questioned.

"Yes, of course. I believe they are still by the front desk. Come, I'll show you." The doctor escorted John out the room with the nurse.

Castel sat back down, looking again at Cherry. She didn't know what to feel. What if Cherry went to jail? Would they question her about the drugs in her system? Castel put her face in her hands and began to sob quietly. "Why God? Why?" She felt like each piece, of her once golden life, was quickly being chipped away.

Castel stood in her room getting dressed for the first day of the school year. Her baby bump was becoming evident, but she still hadn't told her parents. She dreaded telling them. Despite their hectic schedules John and Mirah were active and involved parents. John was the chief of police and the most honored cop in his division, and Mirah was the top OB-GYN in Atlanta, but neither was ever too busy to notice there own baby was going to have a baby. Castel knew it was only a matter of time before they caught on.

She stared at herself in the mirror, rubbing her growing stomach. Tears started to roll down her cheeks but this time she let them fall. "How could I have let this happen?" she asked, aloud. "This was supposed to be my last year of school." She continued to cry as she sat on the edge of the bed. Her tears fell harder as she thought of all her hard work going down the drain. She knew she would have to take time off from school and that would ruin her plans of early graduation. She could kiss her college scholarships away and her position on the cheerleading team goodbye. The reality, of all of her ambitions fading away, chipped away at her deeper and deeper. On top of all of that, Dante was still refusing to talk to her. When she called, voicemail always picked up. She would text, but never got an answer. When she went to his house, his father covered for him, saying he would tell Dante that she came by. Dante's behavior was the unbearable dagger in her back. She wanted his support. She needed his support to give her the extra strength to get through this. Castel put her head in her hands as she continued to sit on her bed. She let the rest of her tears trickle down her face and cover her palms. She wiped them on her pants, exhaled, and then grabbed her stuff for school.

She made her way to the living room where Sylvia, the housekeeper, was dusting the furniture. She stopped and greeted Castel as she entered the room.

"Good morning, Dear. How are you?" Sylvia asked. Her sweet elderly voice kissed Castel's cheeks.

"Blek! That's how I feel, Sylvia. Blek! Can't I just stay home for another two months?" Castel whined, as she leaned on Sylvia's shoulder.

"Don't you mean for another nine months?" Sylvia inquired, as she gently tapped Castel's growing bump.

Castel jumped away from Sylvia's comforting shoulder and made a funny face. Sylvia made one back at her. The two had always had a beautifully close relationship. The housekeeper had been with the family since Castel was three and there wasn't anything Castel couldn't tell her. Besides Cherry, Sylvia was the only one who knew about her pregnancy and was helping her keep the symptoms down and covered up from her parents.

"Did you remember to take all of your vitamins this morning Dear? You don't need to be in that school all tired and giving others something to talk about," Sylvia told her, as she pinched her nose.

"Yes, I took all of my vitamins and don't worry, the last thing I'm trying to do is give any of those nosey heads my name for gossip," Castel assured her with a sassy neck roll.

Sylvia smiled at her. "You know…I can't wait until you finally tell your parents. I know they'll be filled with joy, Dear," Sylvia encouraged, as she fixed Castel's curly long hair.

Castel bit the inside of her mouth. The last thing she believed was them being filled with joy. It was more likely to be disappointment or blind fury. She dropped her head, but Sylvia picked it back up and looked into Castel's hazel eyes.

"Now, don't you start any of that pouting? You'll be fine, so just cut out all that boo hooing. Ok? She gave Castel her lunch bag and walked her out the door. Castel gave Sylvia a huge hug before finally heading off. Instead of driving her car that day, Castel decided to walk to school thinking that maybe it would help to clear her head.

As she walked, she took out her phone to call Cherry. After two weeks in the hospital they had released Cherry. John even managed to get her out of doing jail time for the drug use. She agreed to probation and volunteer work for information on who sold her the drugs.

Castel called twice before Cherry finally answered the phone.

"Hello?" Cherry answered groggily.

"Hello?" Castel replied annoyed.

"Who is this?" Cherry continued.

"Uhhh," Castel cleared her throat. "It's me. I know your butt isn't still in the bed. Did you forget that school starts today?"

"Excuse me, Mother!" Cherry shouted on the other end. "I forgot that it was your job to call and remind me," she snapped.

Castel looked at the phone, shocked at Cherry's response. This was not the first time she had given her a wake up call. She always had to remind Cherry when school was starting up again. "What's wro —" Castel started.

Before Castel could finish Cherry snapped, "Look, I know school starts today. I will get there when I get there, and I will see you when I see you. Now, don't be calling my phone, clocking me," she ordered and then hung up.

Castel stood in the middle of the street trying to figure out what had just happened. Cherry's attitude really just pissed her off. She was far from in the mood to deal with people and their attitudes. She shook her head and continued to walk to school.

Blakedale Vocational High School was full of the brightest and most talented teens in Atlanta, all of which were from different backgrounds. Almost ninety percent of their graduating classes went on to be successful, influential adults, highly known across the south. Castel always wanted to attend this school. Now, in her junior year, she was president of the student government, and captain of the cheerleading squad. Despite all that had happened over the summer, Castel was thrilled to be back in school.

As she walked across the parking lot, she watched for Dante's car. Instead, his friend, Josh bumped into her. Dante and he became friends when they joined the football team together. Even though Castel knew about Josh before he befriended Dante, they hadn't become acquainted until he and Dante started hanging out.

"What's up Crystal Castel?" he greeted with a bright smile.

Castel giggled at the silly nickname and gave him a hug. "What's new? I see you're excited to be getting back into the game," she responded

"You know that! I hope the cheerleaders are twice as ready," he cracked with a small chuckle.

"You always want to come for my squad, don't you?" She shook her head.

"You know I have to. Wouldn't be me if I didn't, but you know it's all jokes. I want to see y'all do your thing this season." He tossed his ball in the air.

"You already know." Castel laughed.

"So you headed to the café? I hear they got a new look and staff. Hope that means they got better grub." Josh smiled as he rubbed his stomach.

Castel cleared her throat. "No, I ate at home. But uh… have seen Dante?" she asked nervously.

Josh stared at her with confusion. He wasn't sure if he should ask about the drama between the two of them or just wait until Dante was ready to give him the whole scoop.

"Hello? Josh? Castel called.

Josh snapped out of his trance. "Nah, you know him. He's not getting here until around ten," Josh replied.

"Yea, you're right. He's not a morning person," Castel said, suspiciously. She could tell Josh was lying, but she knew where his loyalty was. He wasn't going to give up Dante. "Well, okay. I guess I'll catch you later." She smiled and reached for a hug. Castel walked into the school and made her way to the gymnasium. Sitting on the bleachers was the cheer coach, Kira. She spotted Castel from the corner of her eye and stopped what she was doing to greet her as loud as she could.

"Hey Captain Castel!" Coach Kira's voice echoed off the walls.

Castel was glad to see Kira too. She was the big sister she'd always wanted. Kira had taught her everything she knew about boys, and cheering. When it came to those type of topics, Castel always relied on Kira to talk her through them. "Hey, hey Coach Kira," Castel greeted back, as she carefully climbed up the bleachers. She wrapped her arms around Coach Kira and gave her the biggest hug she could. Kira returned the embrace, wrapping her arms tightly around Castel's waist. The pressure on her stomach caused a pain to shoot through her. Castel groaned and Kira let go.

"What's the matter? Don't tell me you've gotten weak over the summer," Kira teased.

"Of course not," Castel laughed nervously. "But we know you have the strength of two men," she smiled, giving Kira a playful nudge.

"Oh, so we've got jokes?" Kira played. "Anyway, we're ready for our new year right? Four year champs? Kira asked.

"Absolutely." Castel's uncertainty was heavy on her voice.

Coach Kira raised an eyebrow. "Listen, don't play with this championship this year. You hear me? If you needed any year to be a champion, it's this year!" The assertion in her voice made Castel's stomach bubble. Kira could see Castel was troubled, but for her, it was too early to deal with teen drama. She picked up her stuff and got up to go to her office. Half way down the bleachers, she turned back to Castel. "Whatever you're going through, better be something that can go away easily. Got it?"

"Yeah, Coach… I got it." Castel's voice trailed off.

Coach Kira continued to her office. Castel was disappointed in the lack of sentiment. She sat for a few more minutes to get the lump out of her throat. The first bell rang and she picked herself up and went to class.

HIDDEN SKELETON

Dante pulled into his reserved parking space at the school. One of the many perks of being the star quarterback. It was already fourth period, but he could care less. He hadn't been feeling well for the last few weeks and was not in the mood to sit in classes. He got out of his car and checked his reflection in the window.

"They should give that spot to me, the way you played at the preseason game." A gruff voice scratched Dante's eardrums. He could see Trey's six foot frame over his shoulder in the reflection. He was the top receiver for the team, but envied Dante's popularity. Though Trey was an amazing player he was hard on the eyes.

Dante turned around with a look of disgust, he had no intentions of changing.

"And to what do I owe this curse?" Dante curled his lip as his words dropped to the ground.

Trey crossed his arms and gave a smirk. "Now, didn't your mother ever teach you to play nice?" Trey teased. Dante snarled. "Down boy." Trey laughed. "All fun and games." He went to go put his hand on Dante's shoulder, but Dane pushed it away. Trey looked at him for a second and then cleared his throat. "Does Coach know his fave is missing out on classes like this?"

"Does Coach know the regular season slacker is out here minding my business?" Dante snapped.

"Oooo, so sensitive" Trey let out a slight laugh and moved closer to Dante. "Your time will soon be up punk. I want to see who's going to sit up your behind then?" Trey smiled.

Dante wished he could shoot bullets out his eyes right then and there. Trey finally walked off and Dante headed toward the school. It felt like rocks were in his stomach, but he shook off his feelings of hate and continued toward the building. He snuck in through the side door. Four years in that school and they still never learned to keep it locked. Halfway down the hallway and he was stopped by security.

"So we're starting early this year, huh?" Mrs. Otis asked.

Dante let out a sigh. "Clearly." Dante looked Mrs.Otis up and down.

"Don't get smart with me boy! I'm not playing with you this year. You either come to school on time, or you come through the front door, get a late pass, and a write up like everyone else! Got it?" she put her hands on her hips.

Dante exhaled. "Yeah, I got it alright."

"Good. Now get out of my hallway! And I'm not giving you a pass," she assured.

Dante rolled his eyes and proceeded to his locker. Deep down he just wanted to leave, but he knew his father would chew his behind. He got to his locker and slammed his head against it. He was so frustrated he wanted to cry, but that was out of the question. He couldn't do anything he wanted to do. He was everyone else's puppet. He let out a grunt and banged the lockers again. Suddenly, he felt a hand on his back. He turned slightly.

"Hi." Castel's soft voice was comfort to Dante's ears.

He picked himself off his locker. He cleared his throat. "Hey. Where did you come from?" he asked, nonchalantly

Castel smiled. "I was in the art room and I heard the banging." She reached for his hand and rubbed it gently. "What's wrong?"

Her concern seemed sincere. Dante couldn't deny how genuine Castel had always been to him. It made him feel good and at the same time, guilty for how he was behaving toward her.

"Hello?" Castel spoke, breaking his thoughts. "Are you OK, Babe?"

Dante wanted to respond but his pride got the best of him. He snatched his hand away from Castel. "Don't touch me! There isn't anything wrong with me and if there was why would I tell you?" he hissed at her.

Dante's harsh words were too much for Castel. "Dante please. What did I do? How long are you going to be in this mood? I… I just can't deal with it anymore," Castel cried.

Tears welled in her eyes. The salt made her eyes squint. Her knees were weak and her brain was flipping in her skull. She knew she was on the verge of a mental breakdown. She could feel it. Her spirit was plucking the veins from her bones.

Dante looked at the floor. He didn't know what to say; it was as if his words were lost. He raised his eyes back to Castel's face and saw her tears dripping to her breasts, which peaked from her uniform. He opened his mouth to talk, but lost his nerve and instead turned around and walked away, leaving Castel in the hallway.

"Dante!" she shouted, as he disappeared into the stairwell.

He felt like a jerk, but he had no clue what to say to Castel. Making his way upstairs to his class, he found Josh sitting on the ground in the hallway. Dante plopped down next to him.

"Well if it isn't Princess Diana," Josh commented.

Dante cut his eyes. "Don't play with me. What's wrong with the desk in the classroom?" he asked.

Josh let out a soft chuckle. "The desk are fine, it's the teacher to teacher conference I have a problem with."

Dante smiled at their sarcastic behaviors. It's what made their friendship. No one got that part of Dante like Josh. It also help that Josh was always a cool and laid-back guy. He never took anything to heart, which made it easier for Dante to have his moments and not jeopardize their friendship.

"What's your schedule looking like? I have that stupid AP physics class. I'm going to Ms. Johnson after this and —"

"What's going on with you and Castel?" Josh interrupted. "I saw her this morning and ... well ... she was as weird as you when we were at the club. I know you guys are not OK. So, are you going to tell me or what?" he stared at Dante.

Dante exhaled and sat up. He debated if he should tell Josh the whole truth about Castel and him. Part of him was surprised Cherry hadn't spilled the beans. "Um… we're all right," he started.

"Don't lie to me man. You know I don't appreciate that!" Josh's tone became stern.

Dante stared at him for a minute and then turned away. "She's pregnant," Dante finally said, with shame.

"That's great! You guys can get married like you always talked about. What's the problem? Her parents?" Josh inquired.

"It's not mine!" Dante shouted.

"What? What the heck are you talking about? Castel is having a baby a baby and *it's not yours?*" I don't believe you." Josh fanned Dante off.

Dante became annoyed and turned his entire body to face him. "Why don't you ever have my back? Why am I always the one in the wrong to you?" Dante demanded.

"Oooo boy! What did I say now?" Josh scoffed.

"I'm telling you the truth! Her baby isn't mine," Dante assured.

"Says who? Why are being like this about Cas? Come on. We know her better than that. You know the baby is yours!" Josh was annoyed. He couldn't believe Dante was being so cowardly.

Dante stood up and leaned over Josh. "I'll say it one more time, since you seem to have a problem with your hearing. T H E B A B Y I S N O T M I N E!" Dante's words hissed off his tongue.

Josh tossed his stuff to the side and stood up. He was a quiet guy, but he never let others intimidate him. "I don't know what your problem is, but you need to chill," he demanded.

"I don't need to do anything. Your loyalty is all messed up! I tell you a baby isn't mine and you're supposed to back me up! Instead you're making me out to be the bad guy!" Dante's body was hot.

"I'm not your 'yes' man. When you're wrong, I'm going to tell you," Josh informed.

"But I'm not wrong!" Dante yelled.

"Yes you are!" Josh shot back.

"No, I'm not! Cherry told me! She told me the baby wasn't mine!" Dante slipped.

Josh's ears rang. He stared at Dante. "What? When did she say that?"

"That's why you need to be on my side! None of these females can be trusted. Yeah, I thought Castel was different too, but she proved that all girls are good for is a fun time and a bit of information." Dante started to pick up his stuff. He looked back up to see Josh still staring at him with hurt in his eyes. Dante gave him a confused look. "What's your problem? You can't be more upset than me that it isn't my baby?" Dante let out a chuckle and playfully hit Josh on the chest. As he turned to knock on the classroom door to see if they could go in, Josh words hit him.

"You messed with Cherry?" he asked.

Dante turned back around. The look on his best friend's face made him feel the shame of hell. He couldn't speak. He just stared. Josh moved closer.

"Did you sleep with Cherry?" Josh questioned again.

The knot in Dante's throat grew bigger. He could feel the sweat forming on his forehead. He opened his mouth to talk but Josh spoke.

"Loyalty huh? Josh shook his head. He turned around, picked up his stuff, and walked away. Dante stood frozen with Josh's words replaying in his head.

BETRAYAL

Castel picked at her nails as she hid in the bathroom stall. Her spirit was broken. She thought it was just a mood Dante was in before, but now she knew the truth — he didn't want her and he didn't want their relationship. The reality of it all made her clench her teeth. She wanted to cry, but she was out of tears, so she settled for stomping the ground and grunting softy.

"This can't be my life," she expressed. "Why is this my life? What did I do? I thought I was doing everything right? I do well in school. I'm respectful. This isn't supposed to happen to me!" Castel let out another grunt and then heard people enter the bathroom. She recognized the voices of Toni and Laura, two sophomore cheerleaders. They were the only two who'd ever made the team in their freshmen year besides Castel.

"It's so hot in that stupid gym," Toni expressed, fixing her cheerleading outfit. "I wish the school would invest in AC." She turned to Laura and continued, "Can you believe what they are saying?"

"I knew she was fast. Fake little princess," Laura started. "You could always tell, with all the guys who would speak to her."

"That doesn't mean she's fast," Toni chimed in. "You got a point though. But to get pregnant! Now, that's something I didn't see coming."

Castel's stomach knotted.

"I wonder who Coach Kira is going to make captain." Laura continued, as she reapplied her lipstick.

"They'll probably pick one of us. We're just as good as the pretty princess."

They were both laughing until Castel opened her stall door. The girls stared at her fuming face. Toni opened her mouth to speak, but Laura grabbed her arm and rushed her out of the bathroom. Castel was numb. She searched her mind for answers. Who did this to her? Who?

Castel raced down to the gym like a cheetah chasing prey. She bust through the double fire doors, scanning the room. All of the clubs participating in the homecoming were there having meetings about their routines and practices. She saw Dante with the football team, but he wasn't her focus this time. Toni and Laura were bunched up in a corner trying hard not to notice her. In a group by the bleachers, were Cherry and a few other veteran cheerleaders. Castel rushed over. Standing behind Cherry, she tapped her gently on the shoulder. Cherry turned around with an annoyed look on her face.

"Can I help you? Why are you touching me?" Cherry's tone was nasty.

"Can I talk to you please?" Castel's voice was low, but raspy. She wanted to keep her composure.

Cherry cleared her throat. "No. I don't have anything to say to you."

"What's your problem?" Castel raised her voice. "I need to talk to you. Why are you being a bitch?"

"Excuse me? Who you talking to?" Cherry put her hands on her hips, moving closer to Castel. "Remember who you're talking to Princess. I don't want to smack a pregnant woman." The other cheerleaders behind her, smiled and laughed at her comment.

Castel felt a rush of rage devour her. With all her strength she pounced on Cherry, punching her repeatedly as she fell to the ground. The other cheerleaders screamed. The football players ran over to watch.

"Get out the way! Move! Move!" Coach Kira screamed shoving the kids to the side. She grabbed Castel off of Cherry. Castel's hands filled with hair. Cherry's face bruised, with blood trickling from the side of her mouth.

"Get off of me!" Castel roared. "Let me get her! Everything I did for you Cherry!! Everything I ever did for you and this is how you treat me?" Castel kicked and screamed, desperately trying to get out of Coach Kira's arms.

Dante looked on from the other side of the gym in shock. He had no idea who that girl was kicking and screaming in Coach's arms. He turned his head to see Josh staring at him. Josh cut his eyes and left the gym.

Cherry picked herself up off the ground, as she moved her disheveled hair from her face. The students moved out of her way as she stumbled out of the gym. In the hallway stood Josh, who was waiting for her. Cherry tried pushing passed him to get to the bathroom, but couldn't hold her balance. Josh grabbed her, pulling her into the bathroom. He wet some paper towels and gently wiped the drying blood off of her lip. In his arms Cherry was like a puppy. The pit bull that everyone else saw disappeared around him.

She gazed into his eyes. "Why are helping me?" she whispered.

He was quiet. He continued wiping her face with soft strokes, making sure to not bruise her skin with the rough paper towel. When it started to shed, he tossed it in the trash and picked up another wet one from the edge of the sink. As he went to wipe her face again, she stopped his hand. He looked up to meet her eyes. The natural light from the bathroom window bounced off of them. It was like he could see right into her spirit.

"I…I… want to. I like to." His voice was soft, like warm air on flesh.

Cherry began to smile. "Thank you." She brushed his cheek with her fingers as they looked in each other's eyes.

Josh felt the urge to kiss her when the vision of her and Dante came across his mind. His pride kicked in. "I mean, I could see you needed help," he expressed in a rough tone, breaking the trance.

Cherry felt her emotions drop to the pit of her stomach. Josh let go of her body and got off the ground. He washed his hands and started gathering his stuff. He hated being vulnerable around her. She always used it as ammunition. He threw the wet paper towel in the garbage and turned back to Cherry who was still sitting on the ground.

"Are you good now?" Josh asked coldly.

Cherry looked at him in confusion, trying to find a magical answer for his mood change.

"Um… hello?" Josh yelled.

Tears gathered in Cherry's eyes. "What's your problem? I mean we were fine a minute ago and then you just —"

"Please save me the sob story," Josh cut her off.

"But — " she tried.

"No buts. Are we done or not?" His tone became nastier.

"Josh, please, talk to me. This is a time for us," Cherry pleaded, picking herself up off the floor.

"I'm leaving. We're done here." Josh walked to the door, but Cherry grabbed his arms.

"Please. Please don't do this. I need you Josh," Cherry pleaded.

"Let me go!" Josh demanded.

"No. Why are you acting like this?" Cherry questioned, gripping harder on his biceps.

"Get off of me Cherry!"

"No"

"Yes."

"No. I love you."

"Stop saying that." Josh shouted, desperately trying to remove her grip without being aggressive.

"I do. I love you. Please don't do this to me." Tears ran down her face.

"Get off of me!"

"No. Not until you tell me what the problem is. We we're just fine a minute ago. What is wrong with you? You don't treat the one you love like this."

"And you don't mess with your love's best friend behind his back!!" Josh screamed so loud his own ears rang.

Cherry froze with her hands still gripping his arm. She stared in his eyes hoping what she heard was just a lie. "Who told you that? Did Dante tell you that?" Her voice was dry.

"No. I caught him slipping in one of his hissy fits," he snarled. "Of all the people you could have lay down with?" he scolded.

Her ears burned from the disappointment. She shut her eyes tight, letting the remaining tears drop to the floor. Josh hung his head as the silence surrounded them.

"You have completely lost you mind young lady." Coach Kira lectured. Castel finally calmed down and had to face the wrath of Kira. "How do you start a fight in the middle of homecoming practice? You're done. A record of suspension will destroy all your hopes of graduating early," Coach Kira informed.

"But she embarrassed me in front of everyone!" Castel shrieked. Now everyone knows about me and worse they know about that stupid lie." Castel clenched her teeth and closed her eyes tight.

Coach Kira kneeled down beside her and put her hand under Castel's chin, bringing her eyes to meet her. "What stupid lie?" Kira questioned.

Castel's palms started to sweat. "I… I'm um…" Castel stammered.

Coach Kira dropped her head. "Please… Please don't tell me you're pregnant Castel." Coach Kira pleaded. Castel began to cry softly. "How girl? Why? Of all the things you could have done," Coach Kira chastised. Kira picked her head up. "But if you are pregnant then… what's the lie?"

"The stupid lie is that my boyfriend of three years is not the father," Castel informed. She sat back in her chair and crossed her arms.

"That's why you're in such a bunch? Gossip and a stupid little boy you can easily deal with?" Coach Kira scolded. "No one is worth the goals you achieved for yourself. No one can knock you off your path to success. I thought I taught you that." The disappointment in Coach Kira's voice tugged at Castel's heart.

Castel looked at her mentor with sorrow. She had no words to speak. The phone rang. Coach Kira answered with dismay. Castel already knew who it was.

"Coach Kira. Yes, she is here… OK, I'll send her down." Coach Kira hung up the phone and exhaled. She turned to Castel who was biting her lip. "You know where to walk it kid." .

Castel looked down in shame and then picked herself up to walk to the Principal's office. She called herself multiple names as she walked the long hallways to the office. When she got to the door she hesitated, her body sweating. She let out one last long breath and then entered the room.

EXPOSED

Mirah sucked her teeth as she repositioned herself in her seat. "How long is he going to make us wait here?" she whispered in a feisty tone to John.

"Relax. They said he'd be here shortly. He is a very busy man. Give him some time," John explained, as he flipped through a People magazine.

Castel rolled her eyes as she sat across from her parents, scrolling through her phone. Her two- week suspension was finally over and now it was time to face Principal Jerrod. Everyone despised him. There were times he was a really great guy and then other times you really wanted to spit in his eye. Deep down, Castel hoped for the really great guy today.

"I don't know why we had to be here in the first place," Mirah started up again.

"Cas was suspended. Any student suspended must have a follow-up meeting to discuss what the school will do with them now."

"That's what I meant. Castel is one of the top students in this school, if not *the* top! A two-week suspension was ridiculous. Everything she does for this school? Everything we do! I mean it's crazy — "

John cut her off, "Mirah we can't fault the school for Cas's rebellious behavior. She should have known better."

"What?" Mirah expressed with an attitude.

"She knew it was wrong to fight in school. She should have waited to catch Cherry. After all, she knows where she is most of the time. She could have waited and caught her off school premises," John told her pointing to Castel.

"Oh please, John!" Mirah fanned her hand at him. "Like I said, they should have shown a bit of favor toward her — "

"Mom, stop!" Castel interrupted. "There is nothing we can do now. I just want this meeting to be over so I can get back to my regular life. This has been so embarrassing." She sulked and slouched further in her chair.

"Now, cut it out young lady! We don't get embarrassed in this family! If anybody has something to say about you, screw them! You did what you had to do to defend your honor and dignity. Cherry tried to disrespect you and that is nothing we stand for! Especially not from anyone like her. I'm surprised she's still in school," John snarled, as he continued to flip through the magazine.

"John that's enough! No need to bash Cherry," Mirah told him.

"There is every reason to bash her! After what she did to Cas and this family, she deserves another good beating." John admitted.

"Dad! Stop!" Castel demanded.

John looked at Castel with a dazed expression and then turned his attention back to the magazine article. Mirah gave her fiftieth eye roll and stared at the pictures of famous leaders on the wall. Castel exhaled loudly and put her head in her hands. She was tired of the nonsense bickering. It was all she'd heard for the last two weeks. It made her glad to finally be going back to school. Silence covered the office, but was broken by the squeak of Principal Jerrod's door.

"Good afternoon Mr. and Mrs. Rogers. I'm sorry for the wait. Please come in." He gestured toward his office.

Principal Jerrod was a very awkward man. He was always very nervous and seemed unsure of his surroundings. Rumors circulated for years that he actually had a mental disorder, but nothing was ever confirmed. Ironically, whatever his problem was, it did not stop him from being the principal of one of the top schools in the state. Castel always admired him for that.

The family followed each other into his office and sat on the wooden chairs around the table in the middle of his office. "I'm glad all of you could make it," started Principal Jerrod, as he took his seat at his desk. "I will do my best to be as brief as possible. As you know, we are here because of the unfortunate situation that occurred a couple of weeks ago on school grounds. As you are aware, our Code of Conduct considers fighting a red zone violation and we deal with it in the most stringent way, hence Castel's suspension — "

"Excuse me Principal Jerrod," Mirah began in the middle of his sentence. "We are all aware of the unfair and cruel punishment you've given our daughter. Can you please get to the point?" she demanded.

"Her punishment was far from unfair and cruel Mrs. Rogers. It was the exact punishment any student would have receive for such a behavior. A behavior that I was shocked came from Castel," he admitted, looking in her direction.

Castel started to twist up her nose, but remembered who she was sitting in between. No matter how much loyalty her parents had to her, they never would condone disrespect.

"Castel is one of our top students and it has been nothing but a pleasure to have her in our school. However…" he paused, "I've had sometime these last two weeks to go over the incident and the school's policy and I have no choice but to expel Castel from the student body," the principal finished, letting his words bounce off the walls.

Castel's ears rang and her body became numb. Principal Jerrod's words could not be true. Mirah stared back and forth at John and Principal Jerrod waiting for John to blow up.

"But how can I be expelled? You just said I have contributed so much to the school and have always been a pleasure to have as a student. How can you expel me on my first big incident?" Castel asked, with an obvious desperation for answers in her voice.

"Yes Castel that is all true but — " Principal Jerrod started.

"But what? There shouldn't be a but," Castel exclaimed. She wanted to jump across the table and pummel him. What did she have to lose? She was already expelled.

"The offense is just too big for us to ignore," he answered.

"That's crap!" Mirah finally chimed in. "What about Cherry? Is she going to be expelled for causing all of this?" Mirah shouted.

"Actually, due to the fact that Castel attacked Cherry —" Principal Jerrod began

"Oh, you have to be kidding me!" Mirah expressed, falling back in her chair with her hand to her forehead.

"That girl antagonized Castel. She forced her hand," John finally expressed.

"Now you of all people know, John, that when an individual 'pushes our buttons' we can't just go attack them. There are specific laws in the real world and there are specific rules in our school," Principal Jerrod calmly continued to explain.

"So you're telling me that my entire high school career is being washed down the drain, while Cherry gets away scot-free?" Castel cried.

"Again, as I was explaining before, Castel you attacked her. In order for it to be a dual suspension, she would have had to fight back," he explained, with tension building in his throat.

"Well then the school should be held responsible because they are the ones who created these idiotic rules. Wrong is wrong! My daughter should not be the only one getting punished! Especially when she is way better than that slug of a student." Mirah informed, as she sat up in her chair.

"Relax Mirah. You're doing too much," John told her, but Mirah was over waiting for him to take charge.

"This school is disgusting." Mirah hissed.

"Now that is all that I am going to take from you Mirah." Principal Jerrod stood up from his seat. "Considering her actions, I have been nothing but fair to Castel! She got off easy with an expulsion. We were considering pressing charges for child endangerment." He looked at Castel. "If it weren't for your father, expulsion would be the least of your worries."

John sat frozen in his seat. He felt Mirah and Castel's eyes ripping through his flesh. He dared not turn their way. He fixated his eyes on Principal Jerrod who was still standing with his arms crossed staring back at John. He felt no remorse for spilling his guts. John swallowed hard to release his words from the pit of his stomach.

"I think it's time… for us to go," he informed through gritted teeth.

"We won't be going anywhere! You sold out your own daughter? Really, John?" Mirah asked, disgusted.

"I saved her! They wanted to throw her in jail. Child endangerment. That was the charge. She was going to be tried as an adult. I had no choice but to break this deal!" John defended himself, finally standing up from his chair.

Castel looked at her father. She was so disappointed that she barely recognized him. John could no longer take the tearing of her eyes and slowly turned in her direction. No words fell from her mouth. She just continued to stare and shake her head.

"Please don't be upset with John. He only did what any father would do for their child. He did the right thing. You two should be grateful," Principal Jerrod said with confidence.

"You're clearly dumber than you look!" Mirah spit out. "He isn't just *any* father. He is *her* father and as *her* father he should have been in her corner!"

"I was in her corner! How dare you!" John shouted.

"You weren't in her corner. You were in your own. We all know the last thing you want is a negative headline that could tarnish your precious name!" Mirah expressed, as she turned around and stormed out the office.

Castel gave her father one last eye roll and followed behind her mother.

"Cas?" John called, but Castel swiftly made her way to the door.

John and Principal Jerrod followed. Mirah was already half way down the hallway. Castel jogged as fast as her body could take her to get to her mother.

"Castel and Mirah! Stop!" John bellowed.

Mirah quickly turned around in anger. "You don't make decisions here anymore! So don't talk to *me* like that," Mirah shouted.

Castel finally caught up with her mother, who was fuming as she stared at John down the hall. Mirah's face was flushed and the veins in her neck pushed through her tomato skin. She turned around and continued down the hall with Castel behind her.

"Please, everyone, I didn't want Castel's high school career to end this way," Principal Jerrod began, still walking behind

John. "It's unfortunate for all of us. However, at least now Castel can put all her focus into upcoming motherhood," he finished.

Castel almost tripped over Principal Jerrod's words. How did he know? All three of them turned in his direction. Both Mirah and John inched closer to the Principal, who was perplexed by their demeanor.

"What are you talking about? What upcoming motherhood?" John asked in a low tone.

Mirah made her way next to him waiting for Principal Jerrod's response.

"Castel...her pregnancy? Her test results came back positive from her physical. You know? The one she and Cherry took after the incident, to make sure they were both OK. Why else do you think we were going to press child endangerment charges?" he inquired.

"Definitely not for that!" John clarified.

"You're lying. You're a liar!" Mirah accused.

"No. I assure you the results were positive. Coach Kira even confirmed and the test…"

"The test is lying! Coach Kira is lying! You are all liars!" Mirah yelled.

Principal Jerrod clenched his teeth as he realized he was the one delivering brand new information.

Mirah and John turned to look at Castel, whose soft tears stained her cheeks. Mirah moved closer to her daughter, as Castel began to tremble, and gently placed her hand on her daughter's hidden baby bump. Castel became cold. A stunned Mirah whimpered as she rubbed her daughter's growing belly. John stood in the back watching. He was furious. He looked back at Principal Jerrod who stared at the ground.

"We're leaving," John informed in low harsh tone. He turned and walked toward Mirah and Castel. Castel looked at her dad and saw both disappointment and rage in his eyes. "Let's go," he ordered quietly. He removed Mirah's hand from Castel's bump and grabbed them both by the arm. He quickly made his way to the front door exit, pulling them both like disobedient little children. Castel's feet barely touched the ground as she tried to keep up with her father. She looked at her mother who was desperately trying to handle both the situation and the news she'd just received.

They finally got the car and John threw them both at it. Mirah lost her balance and fell into the side door of the vehicle. Castel let out a shriek and kneeled beside her mother to make sure she was okay. Mirah held the left side of her head, which had hit the glass. Castel felt fire in her blood as she looked at the small bump beginning to protrude from her mother's head. She looked up for her father, but John was already sitting in the driver's seat with the car running. Castel shook her head and helped her mother into the back seat. Mirah didn't utter a word. She simply hung her head as the weight of disappointment pushed her down.

Castel got in the front seat, plopping down aggressively and slamming the door.

"Unless you want me to knock you through that door you won't slam it again!" John threatened. Castel stared at her father in disbelief. John cut his eyes and turned his attention to Mirah, who sat quietly in the back. John noticed the bump on her head and her scratched up knees. Guilt began to creep up on him, but he quickly shook it off and brought his attention back to Castel, who dreaded making any further eye contact with him.

"This is your fault," John told her. Castel bit her tongue. "This is all your fault! The expulsion, your mother's pain, that…baby. All your fault!" John hissed. Castel tasted the poison of father's words in her mouth. It made her sick. "You are a disgrace!" John finished, still staring at the side of Castel's head.

Castel felt her palms begin to sweat. She waited for her mother to step in and defend her, but Mirah was like a zombie in the back seat. John put the car in drive and sped out of the parking lot. Castel stared out the window as she wiped away the shame filled tears from her eyes. She watched as the only true home she'd ever known disappeared into the distance.

John sped down the highway all the way home. Castel viciously gripped onto her seat as her father drove like a lunatic.

"John — " Mirah nervously uttered from the backseat.

"Shut up Mirah! I don't want to hear it," John yelled.

"Dad, you're going to kill us," Castel cried.

"You'd be so lucky," he taunted.

Castel looked over at her father, amazed. The man in the driver's seat was someone she'd never seen before. His rage and disappointment completely devoured him. He pulled into the driveway, almost colliding with the garage door.

"Everyone get out my car. Now!" John demanded.

Castel cut her eyes and then got out of the car. She carefully helped her mother out of the back seat, being careful of the bruises. John jumped out the car and stormed into the house.

"Sylvia! Sylvia!" John screamed throughout the house. "Sylvia get in here! Now!"

Castel walked through the front door with her mother by her side. John paced back and forth breathing heavily. "Dad, is all of this really necessary? Why can't we just talk about this? I know I made a mistake, but you're overreacting." Castel's words showed the hurt in her heart.

John was unmoved. He looked back at Castel like a deranged bull. "You don't have a say in this. You did enough when you spread your legs like the whore you are," John insulted.

"John!" Mirah could not believe her husband's words.

Castel's heart raced, her body went numb. Was it really her dad she was talking to? Did he really call her a whore? Mirah stared at the pain in her daughter's face. She tightened her grip and placed her head against Castel's.

Slowly, walking down the steps, Sylvia finally appeared. Her bin of cleaning products was still in her hand. "Is everything OK, Mr. John? You were yelling," Sylvia spoke, keeping her eyes on a tearful Castel.

"Yes I was and if you heard me yelling your name, what took you so long to come downstairs?" John chastised her like a child.

Sylvia dropped her bin to the ground and placed her hands on her hips. She looked over at Castel and Mirah, who still had their eyes fixed on John. Sylvia noticed the scratches on Mirah's leg and forehead. She turned her attention back to

John. "What is your problem young man? And what happened to your *wife*?" Sylvia questioned.

"I'm not a young man Sylvia and this is my family. You should know your place." John's words were sharp. "Now, back to what I needed. Go into Castel's room and clear out everything that's not her bed and any of those fancy labels she loves so much," John ordered.

"And why exactly am I being ordered to commit this little girl into exile?" Sylvia asked, pointing to Castel.

"Little girl?" John almost jumped out of his skin at the comment. "Well Sylvia, let me tell you about this little girl. While her mother and I have been working our butts off, so she could go to the school of her choice, have nice clothes, and live in a wonderful neighborhood in an amazing house, she was out laying down with some boy or boys," John exaggerated.

"Oh, Dad, please! You know who the *one* boy is." Castel was irritated by her dad's attitude.

"You mean that stupid little boy Dante? *That's* who you let knock you up? Great, you'll have his baby and he'll beat it to death before it even reaches five years of age," John ridiculed.

Sylvia's eyes widened at John's words. She looked at Castel and then quickly back to John.

"Can you believe this Sylvia? Pregnant. She is pregnant!" John was frazzled.

"Yes she is…I knew she was," Sylvia admitted.

Time seemed to freeze around them. John's ears buzzed. His heart raced. Mirah swallowed hard as she let her hands drop from Castel. She inched toward Sylvia. "But why didn't you tell us?" Mirah finally asked the housekeeper.

"Because it was something she had to tell you… herself. She didn't need me to parent then. She needed my comfort." Sylvia's words were soft. She looked back at Castel and gave her a small smile. Castel felt her heart warm up. She loved Sylvia's loyalty.

John felt as though his eyes could burn holes in the side of Sylvia's face. His anger lit a fire under his feet. He moved closer to Sylvia and Castel began to panic, but Sylvia continued to stare at her with a smile on her face. John came within a foot of Sylvia when she finally raised her hand to his face to block him.

"Whatever that demon of rage in you is thinking, tell it I'm not the one." Sylvia's New York spirit came through her voice.

John fanned her hand away as they stared each other down. "You have forgotten your place." John told her in a deep whisper. "Get out of my house."

"What? Dad?" Castel was in disbelief.

"Leave me alone Castel." John's tone was hostile.

"John you can't get rid of Sylvia," Mirah defended.

Sylvia and John continued to stare each other down. Sylvia felt a sickening feeling rumble in her stomach. A small voice inside of her dared her to step up and out of her character, but she thought about Castel standing behind her. She turned around to face the sixteen year old who she had helped raise, who was now carrying a bundle of her own. The anguish in Castel's eyes pierced her heart. Sylvia walked toward her and wrapped her arms around her, carefully making sure to squeeze softly. Castel rested her head on Sylvia's shoulder and let her tears roll down her nose.

"You know where you can always find me my dear." Sylvia whispered in her ear.

Castel gripped tighter hearing Sylvia's words. She wanted it all to be a dream. Sylvia gave her one last squeeze and then tapped Castel on the back to let go.

"I'll come back for my stuff. I hope that is ok?" Sylvia asked Mirah.

Mirah looked at Sylvia in shame and then nodded her head yes.

Sylvia gave her a sweet smile and then walked toward the door. Just before she left she turned back and looked at John, his eyes were still filled with rage. She gave him a smile and walked out the door, gently closing it behind her.

CRUSHED BONES

Silence covered the dining room as John, Mirah and Castel sat around the table. The thick awkward air covered them as they let the food get cold. It had been a whole three weeks since Castel was expelled from school and her parents found out about the pregnancy. Castel didn't know which one they were more upset about and she refused to ask. Her father continued to be nothing but nasty each hour of every day.

Castel finally started making her plate as the pains of hunger began to take over her stomach.

"Young lady, if you don't put that spoon down, so help me! I didn't hear anyone say grace at this table." John snapped. He gave her a look of death. Castel put the spoon back in the mash potatoes and bowed her head. John said the prayer.

"Lord, we thank you for this food we are about to consume. We pray you may bless it. We thank you for this day and for forgiveness of our sins and the ungodly sins of others…" Castel gave a side eye. "May you continue to bless us and protect us. In Jesus' name we pray. Amen." John finished.

Castel cleared her throat and continued to fix her plate. Her mother sat across from her motionless. She'd become a zombie through all of this. She'd even taken a leave of absence at work, after she couldn't stop crying during deliveries.

When Castel was finished making her plate she stood up and made her mother's. She made sure to not let any of her food touch. Her mother hated that. She gently placed the plate in front of her mother, unfolded her napkin, and placed it on her lap. John got annoyed.

"What are you doing?" His tone was harsh. "She's not some old senile woman. Leave her alone," John ordered.

"I'm just trying to help her. You know if I don't, she won't eat."

"Had you been more grateful she wouldn't be like this," he hissed.

Castel gave her father a mean glare. She was so tired of him throwing her mistake in her face. She stood up straight, and stared him down.

"Problem?" he asked.

Castel hesitated, still staring. She could feel the fire ready to shoot from her eyes.

"That's what I thought." John chuckled and went back to eating his food. "Now move away from her and go sit. She doesn't need your help."

"I've helped her more in these last few weeks then you have your entire marriage." Castel's words were cold. John froze. Castel stood firm near her mother. John put his utensils down and stood up. Castel could hear his heartbeat, as he slowly moved closer to her.

"Excuse me… Come again?" John asked.

Castel swallowed hard. She knew there was no turning back now. "You heard me. You're so quick to insult me, but you should probably take a good long look in the mirror.." Each word rolled off her tongue like a brick.

"I think this pregnancy is really getting to your head. Now, you're lucky, I'm going to be nice. Sit…down. And that is the last time I'm going to tell you." John's voice was stern.

Castel placed the plate in front of her mother, who still had not moved an inch. She came around and moved closer to her father. She stood in front of him, looked into his eyes and said, "I don't take orders from you…Sir." Castel's breath was cold on John's skin. She backed up and turned around to walk back to her mom, but she felt a rough grip on the back of her neck. John pulled her back to him. Castel gasped and gagged, desperately trying to get out her father's grasp, but his fingers dug into flesh. He pushed her toward the wall. She fought as hard as she could to keep her stomach from hitting.

"Dad, please, my baby. Stop," She cried, but he was another person.

"I don't care about that thing. How dare you talk to me like that. You think you're grown? Huh? I'll show you who the adult is in this house!" John shouted.

He pushed her harder into the wall with both hands around her throat. Castel could feel her eyes bulging out if their sockets. Forced tears ran down her cheek. She slowly started to drift away when she heard a faint scream through the pop in her ears.

"Stop! Stop! Stop!" Mirah shouted, as she leaped at her husband. She punched him over and over again until he finally loosened his grip on Castel's neck. Mirah pushed him into the wall as Castel dropped to the ground, coughing and gasping for air. John stood on the wall with his hands up, ready to block anymore of his wife's punches, but Mirah had stopped swinging. She simply stood in front of John with her fist balled up. Her eyes were bloodshot. She turned and looked at Castel, who was on her side, struggling to keep her eyes open. Mirah kneeled down beside her and placed her hands on Castel's baby bump. Mirah's fingertips gently glided over her daughter's belly. "Are you okay?" Mirah whispered in her sweet voice.

Castel looked into her mother's eyes and started to cry. She swallowed hard. "I'm sorry. I'm... so sorry. This is all my fault," she confessed.

Mirah looked at her daughter with disappointment. She placed her hands lovingly on her cheeks. "No baby. It's ours," she explained, looking back at her husband. "We failed you." Mirah's voice cracked as she turned back to Castel stroking her face. She continued to rub her belly, hoping to feel the kicks of her developing grandchild. "I'll get my kit from the car and check the baby." Mirah assured.

Tears continued to fall from her eyes. Castel slowly turned her head to her father who stared at the ceiling. She noticed his own tears sliding down his cheek. She sat herself up, rubbing the side of her neck. "Dad?" she called. John didn't respond. He continued to look at the ceiling. A moment of silence covered the room.

Mirah sucked her teeth. "John! Can you act like the world doesn't revolve around you for one second?" she chastised.

John gave a side eye. He was ready to be cold and hostile. He cleared his throat and positioned himself for his response, but the look in Castel's eyes made him rethink his words. For the first time he recognized the shame and the disappointment she felt. It was as if she was eight years old all over again and had gotten a "C" on her history report. He had always been a history geek, and she thought he would rip her apart for the grade. Instead he told her how proud he was of her for trying her best. John's thoughts put knots in his stomach. He turned around, ready to walk away.

"John!" Mirah shouted. He froze in place. "What's wrong with you? This is the problem. You never want to talk about things. No one else's emotions matter! It's — "

"Mom, stop!" Castel pleaded. She was over the bickering. She forced herself to sit all the way up. She looked toward her father. She could see the dry blood on his neck from her mother's punches. Immense guilt ran through her. If only she'd been smarter with Dante. She picked herself up off the floor and stepped toward her dad "Why can't we just be kind to each other? Like a family is suppose to be." Castel's voice was tired and hovered over her parent's heads like a plague. "I'm so tired of the fighting. I am *so* tired of the negativity. I don't want to bring a baby into a hostile environment. Please. Please, let's stop this."

Her parents glanced at one another, both waiting for the other to speak. Castel moved closer to her dad and put her hand on his shoulder as she looked back at her mom. Mirah hesitated and then slowly got up off the floor and walked toward her daughter and husband. She stood in front of Castel and gave her a slight smile.

"I'm sorry baby girl. We're sorry." John finally spoke. He rubbed her cheek and then pulled her closer, holding Castel tightly in his arms.

Mirah leaned her body on her husband, gently stroking his head. For the first time, love covered the room. Castel got goose bumps as a feeling of peace filled her. She let out a small chuckle and picked her head up off her dad's shoulder.

"We are pretty weird." Castel laughed.

John and Mirah chuckled and squeezed each other a little tighter. There they stood in the dining room, holding each other lovingly.

Castel quickly put her jacket and sneakers on. She was almost 28 weeks and everything she did was harder and took longer because of her growing baby bump. Her father was able to get her into a night program so she could finish high school and her mother became very helpful with what she needed to prepare for motherhood. The only thing missing now was the most important person, Dante. Her parents finally agreed to confront Brian and Dante on their involvement with the baby and today was that day. Castel finished tying her laces and headed downstairs. Mirah stood in the doorway. "You ready?" Castel asked her mom, placing her hand gently on her back.

"Are you?" Mirah questioned.

Castel bit her lip. "I have to be. He needs to be here for our baby. I can't let him continue to run." Castel gave her mother a smirk and they both walked out to the car where John was waiting.

They each sat silent the whole ride. John pulled into the driveway of Brian's house and Castel instantly felt cramps in her stomach. The whole situation was uncomfortable. Mirah let out a soft sigh as John roughly cleared his throat. No one knew the outcome of the upcoming conversation.

"Ok, let's go." John asserted.

Mirah got out and opened the door for Castel, but she didn't move. She was like a mannequin. Mirah looked at her with confusion. John noticed his wife's face as he stood on the other side of the car. He bent down to look in the window to see what had her stuck and there he saw Castel, still in the backseat. John let out a strong sigh and walked to her side. He gently moved Mirah away from the door and reached his arm out to Castel. His touch broke her trance as she fought back her tears.

"This is your call baby girl. Whatever you want to do now is all you." John's voice was genuine and reassuring. Castel gave her dad a soft smile and a hug as she stepped out of the car. Castel was afraid of the outcome, but her parent's support gave her strength. They led the way to the front door, where she paused for a minute and then with her fist she banged on the door until she heard heavy footsteps coming her way. The door swung open. There stood Brian, dressed in black, Old Navy, sweats with a look of disgust on his face.

"Why are you knocking on my door like that pretty princess? Your father may be police, but you definitely don't live here." Brian spit his words out like venom.

"Now, you're going to respect my daughter while I'm standing here!" John assured. "She's never disrespected you, so check yourself!" John demanded.

Brian gave John a stern look and stepped out of the doorway. "First off, what you're not going to do is come at me like that on my property. So you check yourself, because if I recall, I did catch miss loose goose one day getting busy in my house. Some might call that disrespectful." Brian's words were sharp.

Castel swallowed hard. She couldn't believe he said that in front of her parents. She was too ashamed to turn around and look at their faces. Mirah felt Castel's shame in the air and placed her hand on her daughter's shoulder.

"We are clearly aware of the decisions our daughter has made in the past, but that's not why we are here. We want to talk about the outcome of the those actions," Mirah explained, as she rubbed Castel's protruding belly.

"Exactly." John chimed in. "That's the only reason we're here. To discuss how Dante and you are going to help with the baby."

"Dante and who? Last time I checked I didn't lay down with anyone and make a baby, so I won't be helping with anything."

"But this is your grandchild and we don't expect Dante to know how to do everything on his own." Mirah said.

"That all sounds personal and according to my sources that's not my grandchild." Brian smirked, as he leaned on the wall.

"I resent those stupid rumors." John hissed.

"You're an adult Brian. The last thing you should do is listen to a bunch of gossiping teenagers." Mirah rolled her eyes.

Brian raised an eyebrow. "You're right. I shouldn't listen to gossiping teenagers, but one person I will be listening to is my son. I'll support what he supports, so let's see what he says."

"Let's." Castel spoke.

Brian looked at her with disgust and then led them into the house. With a harsh gesture he showed them to the den. He called for Dante, who was upstairs in his room. Castel could here the slow jams of R&B blasting through the walls. The memory of Dante always trying to sing his favorite tunes to her made her smile. She said a little prayer to herself, hoping her time away from Dante had helped him get his mind right. She snapped out of her trance before anyone noticed, but they were all too busy in their own worlds regardless. Mirah picked at the skin on her nails, something she did when she was nervous, but it was a horrible habit for someone who delivers babies. John was busy giving Brian dirty looks as Brian sat at his bar making himself a drink.

Brian was aggressively putting the bottles and glasses back. Castel rolled her eyes at their pettiness.

"And they wonder where their children get it from," she thought.

Just as she started to lean back in the chair and relax, she heard Dante coming downstairs. She straightened back up and fixed her eyes on the staircase. She froze at the sight of him. The young man she fell in love with was no more. Dante looked almost thirty pounds thinner. His bulging muscles had disappeared. His glowing, clear, skin was dry and bumpy. He was clearly weak and exhausted. John and Mirah stood up shocked at the sight. Dante looked at them with anger. He hated being judged. He turned his attention to his dad.

"Yeah, Dad? What's up?" Dante asked. His voice was groggy and low.

Brian ignored the obvious reactions from Castel and her family and addressed his son. "You've got company. They insisted they see you." Brian's sarcasm was bitter as it dripped from his lips.

Dante rolled his eyes as he turned his head back in the direction of Castel and her family. "Can I help you?" Dante asked harshly.

Castel and Mirah continued to stare. John waited for them to snap out of it and then cleared his throat to speak. "We need to talk about the baby."

"What baby?" Dante asked with hostility.

"This baby," John said, pointing to Castel's round belly. "The baby you created with my daughter. The baby she is carrying for the both of you!"

"I don't know if anyone has informed you, but that's not my baby," Dante asserted, as he put his hand in his pockets.

"Dante… don't do this," Castel finally spoke.

"The only thing I'm doing is speaking the truth," Dante told her.

"Little boy, now you listen here to me — " John began.

"Little boy?" Dante interrupted.

"Yes! Little boy! What you're not going to continue to do is disrespect my daughter. She has been nothing but good to you. My wife and I have been nothing but good to you. This is not how you show gratitude." John's tone was strong. "I don't want to keep hearing about some stupid rumor that was created by some two-faced friend who can't find her left from her right her darn self." John told him.

"Well the last time I checked, birds of the same feather, flock together." Dante hissed.

"Excuse me?" Mirah finally spoke. "Dante what is wrong with you? This is not the young man that we know. You have never spoken to us in such a manner and to talk about Castel in such a way. Look what has become of you. I mean… what is wrong with you?" Mirah asked.

Brian's blood boiled at Mirah's words. He moved Dante to the side. "The stress of this nonsense is what is wrong with him. Ever since he found out about this stupid pregnancy his game has been off," Brian scolded. "He can't focus. He's sick all the time. He's lost three scholarships! That's his future right down the drain. But do you care? No! All you want him to care about is that stupid baby," Brian hollered.

"His stupid baby!" Castel screamed as she pointed to Dante. "He's not the only one who's suffered. He's not the only one who has taken losses. I got kicked out of school! Embarrassed by the man I love and by my best friend! So don't tell me about losses!" Castel's roar echoed throughout the house. She stood fuming, ready to pounce. Mirah took a step toward Castel and placed a hand on her head. Mirah's touch calmed Castel's spirit. She put her hand down, but didn't take her eyes off Brian. Dante walked over to his father and stood in the middle of him and Castel. He looked deep into her eyes.

"Like I said, that's not my baby. I don't want anything to do with it or you," Dante told her in a soft yet cruel tone. "Go away and leave me alone... for good." He then turned and walked towards the stairs.

"If you're not going to take responsibility voluntarily we will have to deal with this the legal way," John threatened.

"Do your worst." Dante told him, as he continued up the stairs.

Brian went to the door and held it open. "Goodbye and thanks for the visit." His voice dripped with sarcasm.

They all walked towards the door. Mirah consoled Castel as she began to cry softly. John walked behind his girls. Before stepping out the door he turned back to Brian. "I'll have my lawyer call you." John assured him.

"I'll be waiting." Brian closed the door behind him and paused before going to the phone. He scrolled through his contacts and dialed a number.

"Hi Brian." Lorena answered. "To what do I owe this pleasure?" she asked.

"Cut the cute stuff Lorena. Our boy is in trouble.

SELF DESTRUCTION

Cherry lay in her bed, picking at an old scab from her needle marks, flinched at the pinching pain that gave her an odd satisfaction. She smiled softly, but became annoyed as her middle aged customer grunted next to her. She rolled her eyes and looked at him with disgust. She hated how she used her body, but knew there was no other choice. It was either sugar daddies or retail, and that was a struggle she refused to live.

Getting out of bed, she headed to the bathroom to jump in the shower. She let the water run for a few minutes to make sure it was burning hot. Cherry loved when the burning water pierced her skin. It was as if each of her scars and pains were being carved away. She closed her eyes and imagined disappearing to an unknown place, away from everyone and everything. As she reached for her loofa she felt a soft blubbery wall blocking her.

"Ready for breakfast?" A deep raspy voice asked.

Cherry opened her eyes to see her customer standing in front of her. The sight of the water disappearing in his rolls and down his body made her sick. She stared at him annoyed.

"What's wrong?" he asked.

"Why are you in my shower? Aren't you supposed to be getting dressed?" Cherry questioned.

"Don't act like that. I thought we could get one more in before I went back to my wife," he finished, as he smiled and jiggled his body. He moved forward, but Cherry shoved him away and jumped out the shower. She grabbed her towel and dried herself off.

"What's you problem? I pay good money for you. You wouldn't have any of this if it weren't for me!"

"You pay good money for dinner and dessert, not breakfast and I have all of this because your wife doesn't do what I do," Cherry snapped. "Now, get your big behind out my shower and get out of my house!" Cherry told him. She stomped out the bathroom and into her room to grab her robe. Her customer left the shower and followed her.

"You don't tell me what I paid for! I give you money. You give me what I want until I say no!" he demanded.

Cherry chuckled, "I can see you've forgot how this goes. You don't call the shots when you already gave me the money. Like I said, you paid for dinner and dessert. Unless you're increasing my allowance, which I doubt according to the conversation I heard you have with your accountant last night, there is no breakfast."

"Like I said, I want it. Now you either give it to me or I take it." He walked toward her with his fists balled up.

Cherry laughed and walked over to her nightstand. She pulled out a .9 caliber and pointed it at him. "You really did forget how this goes. Been in California so long, playing the family man, you forgot how I do things," she said, guiding the gun down to his genitals.

His body froze as the cold metal touched his skin. Cherry found the fear in his eyes enticing. She pushed the gun closer. He jerked with fear.

"Please… I'm sorry. I'll leave right now," he pleaded.

"Too late for that. That's the problem with you selfish humans. You think everything works on your time. But nothing is given to you in this world. There is a price to pay for everything," Cherry spoke through clenched teeth. "I didn't give you a good time… you paid for it. You didn't give me money." She leaned in closer. "I worked for it." The man trembled with fear. Cherry was slowly going insane.

"Please. Please don't kill me. I just want to get back to my wife," he pleaded again. His words pissed Cherry off even more.

"Your wife? That's what you really care about, huh?" Cherry asked. "Your stupid wife! What happened to caring about me? I've given you my body, my soul, and all you want to do is go back to that stupid wife?" Cherry screamed, backing up from the terrified middle-aged man. "I am so tired of you men. I am so tired of being used. I have feelings too! What does she have that I don't have? Huh? Tell me Dante! What does Castel have that makes you love her more than me?" Cherry cried.

"I…I'm not Dante," he stammered. "Who is Castel?"

Cherry stood silent with her mouth open. She put the gun down and backed away with her eyes still focused on him. "Get out," she whispered.

"What?"

"Get out! Get your stuff and get out of my house!" Cherry yelled. She picked his things up off of the floor and threw them at him. He moved as quickly as possible, throwing on his pants and grabbing what he could. He ran down the steps with his things in his arms, with Cherry chasing behind him. As he swung the front door open, there was Josh on Cherry's front step.

"Who are you?" Josh asked. "Cherry are you okay? What the heck is going on?" Josh stepped in the door.

"What are you doing here Josh?" Cherry asked with an attitude.

"Please… I just want to go home. I don't want anything to do with this." The man pleaded.

The mere sight of him angered Josh. "You don't want anything to do with this and yet here you are. A grown man, half-naked, with a half naked seventeen year old… I wonder how the police would feel about that," Josh snarled.

"Mind your business Josh!" Cherry scolded.

"She told me she was twenty-five. She played me," the man explained.

"Oh please! Whether I was seventeen, twenty, or twenty-five you didn't care. You were just glad someone like me wanted to lay down with you."

"Shut up Cherry," Josh said. He got closer to the man and looked deep into his eyes. "If I ever catch you in this house again, or anywhere near here again, I'll make sure when they lock you up that she wasn't the only one wanting to lay down with you. Got it?" Josh's voice was hostile and shaky.

The man shook his head yes and then jetted out the door. Josh closed the door behind him and as he turned around Cherry landed a burning slap across his face.

"Who do you think you are? Don't you come through here kicking out my customers. Especially when you don't pay the bills around here," Cherry scolded, as she put her hands on her hips.

Josh rubbed his face and looked at Cherry with disappointment. She forced herself not to look at him. He stepped closer to her. "What's going on with you Cherry? I thought you got past this? I thought you wanted to do better?" Josh asked.

"I did! Then those who promised to be by my side left me hanging, so I had no choice but to do what I needed for me," Cherry expressed, nonchalantly.

"Oh please, Cherry, cut your crap. No one left you. Yeah, I promised to have your back if you did what you told me you were going to do. Remember? You said you were going to put the old geezers and bad habits behind you, but every time I gave you money for bills, I found you giving it to the local dealer!" Josh blasted. "You remember that? And now look, once again I catch you doing something — "

"Ooooo Josh shut up! I am so tired of you and all your stupid judgments!" Cherry yelled. "I do, what I do, to make sure I'm good, point, blank, period. No one has ever looked out for me just because! I always have to do something in return. I ask for help to do better, I need to do it on your terms. I ask for good friends, Castel only keeps me as a friend as long as she can walk all over me. I ask for help when I'm sick and all she does is lecture me like she's my mother. She thinks she is so much better than everyone else. Oh, and that stupid local dealer you're talking about, made me do him and two of his friends just for a twenty dollar bag of hero. Like, are you kidding me?" Cherry exclaimed. "I am so tired of everyone! When is anyone going to love me? When is anyone going to have my back?" Cherry cried. The salty tears dripped from her lips.

Josh looked at her and in a moment of weakness wanted to hold her like he would have in the past, but a small voice in his head told him not to. He took a deep breath and said, "You're pitiful Cherry. All you do is want someone to feel sorry for you. When was the last time you asked me about my day? How is school? How am I doing? Huh? When?" Josh asked. "All you do is call when you need something and I still always have your back. Not once have you ever given me a simple thank you. You're just as selfish and just as much of a user as all the people you mentioned!" Josh finished.

"I hate you. I…hate…you." Cherry said.

Josh felt his body get hot. "You don't hate me. You hate yourself." Josh was no longer going to let Cherry bully him with her words.

Cherry lifted her hand to smack Josh again, but this time he blocked her and pushed her away. She stumbled over her boots and fell into the wall. Gathering herself, she looked at

Josh in shock. He had never been that aggressive, and she was surprised that he showed no remorse.

He kicked Cherry's boots to the side as he moved toward her. "You are the selfish one," he repeated. "You think you're the only one who has no one to call or depend on? I've been bounced around since I was a baby too Cherry." The frustration in Josh's voice escalated. "I didn't understand what home meant until my Aunt took me in at the age of eight, but that was short lived when the state gave custody back to my mom when I was ten. She only managed to stay sober for a few months and then she was right back on the streets junked up!" Josh shouted.

Tears fell from Cherry's eyes. She felt more worthless than ever. Josh kept his stance, still standing over Cherry. "I did what I needed to do too, Cherry, but not at the expense of my integrity. No one owes you anything in this world and you have to learn to accept that." He stared Cherry in the eyes and could see she was filled with shame. She stood up straight and reached for him, but he turned and walked to the door.

"Josh…" Cherry called. "Please… I'm sorry. Don't leave me… not like this. I'll change. I will. I just need you to help me this one last time," she pleaded.

Josh turned back to face her. "You don't need me. I can't help you. You have to learn how to help yourself. How to love yourself." Josh's voice drifted. He stroked Cherry's cheek gently and wiped her tears. Josh's touch gave her chills. She grabbed his hand and pushed it harder to her cheek as if she wanted him to become part of her. Josh desperately wanted to give

Cherry all the help she wanted him to give, but he remembered from his mom how much of a waste that was. He knew she had to want better for herself. He pulled his arm away from Cherry and went back towards the door. Cherry called for him one last time, but her words dropped to his feet as he closed the door, leaving her in the foyer.

Cherry stood in the silence. She felt her emotions creeping up on her. The feeling made her sick. She closed her eyes tight thinking it would help the feeling disappear. Images of her parents popped in her mind, the words of her aunts, and the sweet voice of her grandmother.

"Nana,…" she spoke out loud.

The memory of her grandmother shredded every emotion left in her spirit. Her knees weakened. Just as she wanted to fold into a ball and cry. The urge for a hit took over her body. She shook off her sorrow and headed upstairs, where she threw on the rest of her outfit and rummaged through her drawers for her money. She secured $150 dollars in a rubber band and shoved it in her bra before grabbing her keys and heading out the door.

Down the back streets she sped until she approached an old town house. Whoever the owner was had long stopped taking care of it. Cherry pulled up in front of the rusted gate and beat up sidewalk. She adjusted her outfit and got out of her car. She slowly strutted up the stairs and rang the rusting doorbell three times.

"Who ringing the bell like they live here?" A hoarse voice shouted from the other side of the door. The door flung open and there stood a scruffy middle-aged man with a black n'mild hanging from his lip. He was dressed in a long, plain white, tee shirt that touched his knees. He was a couple of inches shorter than Cherry, but built like a rock. His name was Reck.

"Well, well if it isn't Cherry pie." He took a sharp inhale from his mild. "Where you been hiding?" he asked, leaning forward.

Cherry scrunched up her face and proceeded to walk past him, but he put his arm out to block her. "You got a problem Reck?" Cherry questioned with attitude.

"Yeah I got a problem. You not just walking up in here like we cool with you?" he informed.

"And is there a reason y'all not cool with me?" Cherry pushed his arm and stepped inside the house.

"You stupid little — "

"Reck!" A voice yelled from upstairs. Down the steps he came. One of the top street hustlers in town and Cherry's supply man. Sly was six foot one with a shiny bald head and a thick black beard. His caramel skin was enviously clear and his teeth were the nicest and straightest Cherry had ever seen. On the last step he stood staring Reck down for creating a scene. Reck looked down at his shoes, trying hard to brush off Sly's death stare. Cherry smirked on the side, loving every minute of Reck putting his tail between his legs. She couldn't believe his attitude toward her and she wanted Sly to dig into him real good.

Sly stepped down and came within inches of Cherry and Reck. He leaned halfway toward Reck and whispered. "I got this." His voice was calm and Reck looked up at him and gave a small nod. He then closed the door and gave Cherry a look of disgust before walking off to the next room, down the hall.

"That's it? You're just going to let him try me like that?" Cherry sneered. "What was his problem anyway?" she asked, as she walked in the direction of the living room. Just as she took her purse off her shoulder to place on the torn leather couch, she felt a blow to the back of her head. She stumbled before dropping to her knees. The sight of stars and colorful lines filled her vision and she held her head and cringed in pain. She turned around and another blow hit her in the face. Her entire body hit the ground.

Sly kneeled down next to Cherry as she moaned in agony. "You always got a big mouth, always the slick talker, but this time you're going to pay for it." Sly moved Cherry's hair from her face, revealing a red swollen mark.

Cherry stared at Sly with the deepest fear in her eyes. A tear trickled down her cheek, but Sly gently wiped it away.

"What's wrong Cherry pie? I thought you were Miss Big and Bad? Miss Fearless? You real scary now, huh?" he taunted.

Cherry swallowed the spit in her mouth and pushed her words past the lump in her throat.

"What… did I …do?" Cherry's voice was like a child.

Sly gave her a look of sympathy and then sat down next to her. He took a five inch pocket-knife from his side and flicked it open and closed. Cherry's entire body went numb with panic and her eyes widened.

"You see Cherry Pie, when you run your mouth, the words you spit out always come back to Sly's ears." He used the knife to point to his head.

Cherry stared in confusion. "This is because of what I said to Reck? I've talked to him like that before and it's never been a problem," Cherry explained.

"Don't play with me! You know that's not what I'm talking about. You sent the cops after me didn't you?" Sly's voice elevated.

Cherry tensed up even more. She ran through her mind, trying to think of what he could possibly be referring to and then she remembered her deal to get probation. Her heart skipped a beat. How did Sly get involved? She never gave his name specifically. She gave some other nickel and dime hustlers in the area, who she got her sour from.

Sly quickly jabbed Cherry in her thigh and woke her up out of her trance. Cherry clutched her thigh in agony, but it only made the blood ooze out of the wound quicker.

"I want to hear it come out of your mouth Cherry Pie! You sent those cops didn't you? Last time I checked, you're the only one whose bestie's father is the Chief of Police."

"No Sly, please. She's not like that. I didn't — " Cherry eagerly wanted to explain, but Sly made up his mind and punched her directly in the mouth, cutting her off in mid sentence. Cherry grabbed her mouth with a quickness trying to deal with the pain. Sly stood up over her and watched her jerk in agony.

"Next time you'll know to keep your once pretty little mouth shut," Sly informed.

Cherry looked up at him in terror. Just as she tried to fix her lips for one more explanation, Sly threw a kick to her side as hard as he could. Cherry screeched as Sly kicked her again. He grabbed her by her hair and dragged her across the floor. She tried to beg, but her efforts were pointless. He continued to beat her as her screams of help drifted into the distance.

THE FALLEN KING

"I can't believe what the heck you're saying," Brian expressed. Lorena had finally shown up to go over a strategy in order to be ready for anything John was planning to throw their way, but she was refusing to see the right in Dante's actions.

"Why would you expect me to agree with this nonsense you're telling me? He laid down to make a baby, but is refusing to take care of it and you expect me to defend him? Are you crazy?" Lorena explained.

"I didn't make a baby! The child is not mine!" Dante expressed

"Oh, boy, please! I see adult men tell me that all the time when they're taken to court for a paternity test, just to stand in the courtroom with their foot in their mouth when the test comes back positive," Lorena explained, waving her hand at Dante.

"Would it kill you to support your son one time in his life Lorena? Would it? You can't do anything else. This one time he needs you the most and he still can't depend on you!" Brian criticized.

"Don't start that nonsense with me Brian. You two only want me to support things that are beneficial to you. Any other time I'm given the cold shoulder," Lorena told him.

Brian moved in closer to Lorena. Dante backed away. He knew when his father got quiet it was never good. Brian gave Lorena a cold look. "You will do this for him. I've worked countless hours for eighteen years to see him have a bright future. You will *not* screw it up." Brian's voice was assertive.

Lorena's body got tense. She moved in even closer, unwilling to fold under Brian's aggression. "And I am not the teenager you impregnated eighteen years ago. You don't intimidate me anymore Brian," she assured him. "I'm not helping our son get out of this, but it's nice to see the apple doesn't fall too far from the tree," Lorena said, crossing her arms.

Dante frowned his eyebrows from curiosity. Brian's intensity softened.

"What does she mean?" Dante asked looking at his dad. Brian ignored Dante and continued staring down Lorena, who had a smirk on her face. Dante stepped toward his parents. "What are you two talking about?"

"Nothing," Brian finally spoke. "Your mother was always more concerned about being a feminist than being a good mother," Brian sneered.

"How dare you!" Lorena snapped. "I'm not a good mother because you had to step up and be a father to *your* son? This is not the 1900's. I don't have to be barefoot and pregnant!" Lorena scolded.

"There you go again! He's always just my son. Never ours. I didn't push him out, you did! You'd think you'd care more!" Brian shouted.

Dante rolled his eyes. He went to the front closet and grabbed his sweater. He would rather be anywhere than here right now. He left the house, softly closing the door. He refused to interrupt their quarrel. It would be too much to think they would actually care about where he was going.

Dante walked down the street toward the basketball court. Memories of when he was a child, sneaking out the house to play a few games with his friends filled his mind. He never won any of the games. Basketball just wasn't the sport he was gifted in.

As he got closer to the gate he could see Josh shooting hoops by himself. He hesitated for a minute then walked across the court to him. Josh was clearly in a tense mood and the sweat stains on his clothes showed he'd been there for a while. Josh let out loud grunts and bounced the ball as hard as he could. He threw it at the hoop, not caring if he made any shots or not. Dante approached with caution. He hadn't talked to Josh since that day at school. Anytime he tried calling, it went straight to voicemail.

"Yo." Dante called with hesitation. Josh snapped out of his trance and turned to Dante. "What's up?" Dante asked, like nothing was wrong. Josh gave him a look of disgust and continued throwing the ball. Dante instantly became annoyed and let out an aggressive sigh. "Yo, you wack you know that?" Dante shouted.

"Excuse me?" Josh caught the ball and turned around to address Dante.

"You heard me! You wack! We've been boys for how long and this is how you're going to act over some chick?" Dante insinuated.

Josh moved closer to the gate and in an act of rage threw the ball at Dante. "Don't tell me how to act, and don't come at me like I'm the one being disloyal! You're the one who can't be trusted!" Josh yelled. "She wasn't some chick. If I'd just met her then she may have been some chick." He shook his head. "But, Cherry, son?" Disbelief rang in his voice. Josh truly didn't want anything to do with Dante at this point. He went and picked up his ball and continued throwing it at the basketball hoop.

Dante hung his head in guilt and then walked around the gate to the entrance to get closer to Josh. He looked at him throwing the ball over and over again. Each throw was more aggressive than the last one. "Ok… Ok. You're right. I messed up," Dante admitted. Josh froze, but kept his back to Dante. "I messed up. You're right. That was your girl. That was my girl's best friend. I was being selfish. I — "

"Yo, you're good." Josh cut him off. "You're good. I'm… I'm not stressing it. We're good." He was never into talking about his emotions, and after his conversation with Cherry he was on an emotional shut-down.

"You want to shoot some ball?" Josh asked, desperately wanting to change the subject.

Dante smiled. "Nah. This basketball thing is all you. Never me."

"I know, that's why I'm asking you to play." Josh joked.

They gave each other a smile. "Nah. I'm good." Dante rejected again, as he sat down on the ground. Josh joined him. They sat in silence, both searching their minds for words. Josh couldn't help but notice Dante's new appearance. He'd never seen him that drained. Josh felt an urge to question him, but he resisted, not wanting to start another argument. Dante felt Josh's stares piercing his skin.

"So what's up with you?" Dante asked, looking to stop any questions he thought Josh was getting ready to ask him.

Josh got the message. "Shoot. A whole bunch of things," he confessed. "I went to see Cherry to find her kicking out one of her stupid sugar daddies," Josh told him, shaking his head.

Part of Dante wanted to be petty and ask Josh why was he surprised, but he knew it was too soon to crack jokes. "That's crazy. I thought she gave up that life?" Dante expressed, forcing himself to sound concerned.

"Yeah me too. Then she has the nerve to blame me. Saying, if I had just taken care of her, like I promised, she wouldn't have to turn tricks. Can you believe that crap?" Josh scoffed. "I'm done with her. She wants to keep digging a grave, I'll let her keep digging it. I've got too many great things happening to me right now."

A knot formed in Dante's throat. He couldn't help but be envious of Josh's accomplishments. Three of the top schools for basketball already offered him full rides and he heard that a scout from the NBA wanted to fly him out to California to meet with him. Josh was achieving all the things he planned to achieve for himself. It sucked to see someone else living his dream, even if it was his best friend.

Josh realized Dante was in a daze. He picked up his ball and gently tossed it at him, hoping to snap him out of it. "You alright?" Josh asked.

Dante forced a laugh and tossed the ball back. "Yeah I'm good. Just a lot on my mind. You know... with all the things going on with the baby," he lied. "You bringing up Cherry made me think about that crazy best friend of hers. She'd driving me crazy with all the baby needs and cravings."

"Oh, so you guys are good now?" Josh asked, surprised.

"Yeah we're good. It's just a lot. It's stressing me out. Got me all out of whack." Dante chuckled awkwardly.

"Yeah I can see that," Josh spoke, regretting it instantly.

Dante gave him an annoyed look, which caused Josh to hang his head in embarrassment. An awkward silence lingered between them. Josh searched his mind for something to cut the thickness, but was saved by the ring of Dante's phone. Dante hesitated in answering it. God forbid it was Lorena, his dad, or worse Castel. He just sat and let it ring. Josh looked at him with confusion.

"Why don't you want to answer the phone?" Josh questioned.

"I'm not really in the mood to talk to anyone," Dante admitted.

Josh gave him a suspicious look. "But you didn't even look at the phone. Were you expecting a call? Is it somebody you don't want to talk to in front of me?" Josh asked.

"What? No... I don't care who it is. I don't want to talk to anyone right now," Dante explained. He didn't understand where Josh was going with all his questions. Josh looked away insulted at the idea that Dante was lying to him. Dante let out a sigh and took his phone out of his pocket. He opened it to see a missed call and a voicemail from Planned Parenthood.

Josh's curiosity grew as he stared at Dante's face. "So? Who was it?" Josh asked, anxiously.

"It's… no one… It's nobody important," Dante stammered.

"It was Cherry wasn't it?" Josh snapped.

"What? Really son? I'm not talking to her! Would you let that go?" Dante answered, annoyed.

"Whatever," Josh replied, brushing Dante off.

Dante shook his head and stood up off the ground. He dusted himself off and adjusted his clothes. "Look I got to go. I'll call you later or hit me when you're in the house," Dante told him, extending his hand for a handshake.

Josh hesitated. "Alright," Josh finally spoke and shook Dante's hand.

Dante quickly exited the court and called his voicemail. His heart raced faster and faster as he walked down the street, punching in the pass code to his voicemail.

"Good afternoon Dante. This is Sandra from Planned Parenthood. I'm calling because your test results came back from your screening and we would like to go over them. Please give us a call back to schedule an appointment."

The words of the receptionist bounced around in Dante's head. What could they possibly want to tell him that they couldn't just say over the phone? What could have possibly appeared on his results that he had to make another appointment? A sense of worry numbed Dante all over. He questioned whether or not he wanted to call them back. He stood in the middle of the street until the honking of the cars forced him on the sidewalk. He started walking and walking, blocking out the existence of everyone around him. Fifteen of what felt like the longest minutes later he was standing at the front door of Planned Parenthood. His sense of urgency picked up and he flung through the door and headed straight to the front desk.

"Yeah they wanted me to come back for something. I'm not sure why." Dante's words were almost gibberish.

The young receptionist stared at Dante with confusion. She turned away from her computer and leaned toward Dante. "Um, OK. Can I have your date of birth, please?" The receptionist could tell this was the last place he wanted to be.

"Why do you need all of that? Look… a woman named Sandra told me I had to come back in. She said I should call to make an appointment, but I'm here already, so tell me what you have to tell me and let me be on my way." Dante's voice carried throughout the waiting room. All eyes were on him, but the worry eating at him kept his attention on the receptionist. He wanted to get his results as soon as possible. He wanted to hear them say it was nothing, or simply something treatable like gonorrhea or chlamydia. Those, he'd admit to. After all, he did have one too many one-night stands.

Dante's commotion caused other nurses to come out from the back. One nurse, Dante noticed instantly. It was Mrs. Sandra, a middle-aged woman, no more than fifty. Dante liked working with her because of all the pictures she had of her patients hanging on her wall. He appreciated the old school wisdom she gave him as she took his information. She noticed Dante as well and gave him a smile.

"Sir we need your information to look you up in the system."

Mrs. Sandra placed her hand on the young receptionist's shoulder. "It's OK Jenna. Here is his name. I'll take him," Sandra assured. She looked back at Dante and gestured for him to come in the back. Jenna rolled her eyes and took the paper. Dante cut his eyes at Jenna's attitude and went to the back. He followed Mrs. Sandra to her office, where her collage of patient pictures hung across the wall. The office had a homey feeling Dante appreciated. Mrs. Sandra caught Dante staring at her pictures. "Maybe one day I can add you up there." She gave him a gentle smile.

It warmed Dante's heart. "Yeah, maybe one day." He leaned toward her, "So… what did my results say," he asked nonchalantly.

Mrs. Sandra's faced dropped and she looked down at his file. She cleared her throat. "Well, your results came back pretty quickly and I remember you were eager to get them back." Mrs. Sandra focused on her papers as she spoke.

Dante noticed her uneasiness. "Yeah, I mean my dad was breathing down my neck to find out if anything was wrong, so I figured I get it out the way. So what did the results say?" Dante asked again, with more alertness.

Mrs. Sandra paused, but then looked at Dante with pity in her eyes. "Your results came back positive." Her voice was low.

Dante swallowed hard. "OK, that's not a real shocker. I mean I knew I had something." He chuckled. "So what it is? The clap? Syphilis? What?" Inside his chest his heart jumped around.

Mrs. Sandra leaned in a bit closer. She looked Dante directly in his eyes. "It was positive for… HIV," she whispered.

Dante heard a loud thump in his ears. His tongue felt swollen and his body froze. "What?" he questioned. There was no way he heard her correctly.

"We'll give you all the necessary paperwork you need to educate yourself about the virus, and all the necessary referrals, so you can get started on the medication. There are a number of support groups you can go to...." Mrs. Sandra went on and on, taking out paper after paper. She avoided staring at Dante any longer, so her own tears wouldn't escape her eyes.

Dante could barely hear what she was saying. It was as if he was hearing her from under water. Mrs. Sandra, reached out and touched his leg, bringing him back to focus. "First things first, however, you have to contact all your sexual partners. I know it will be difficult, but it's protocol. The law…" She had to be sure that Dante heard her. "Son? Dante?" Mrs. Sandra called.

Dante looked right through her. All he could hear were those three letters she read from her paper with his name attached to it. Could it really be what he'd heard? Did she have the right file? There was no way it could be correct.

Mrs. Sandra looked in sympathy as her tears finally escaped from her eyes. Dante caught the sun reflecting in the tears running down Mrs. Sandra's freckled cheek and realized there was no hiding from this.

"H…I…V… I have… HIV?" The world around him quickly crumbled over.

A CRY
FOR HELP

"That color is hideous, Mom. We can't use that." Castel scrunched her face at the frog green decorations her mother loved for her baby shower.

"You need to think outside of the box," Mirah told her. "Green is not just for neutral baby showers. Green for girls can be adorable too." She tried to convince her daughter, but Castel continued to scrunch her face as she looked through the other colors.

"We could always hold on to this color as an option, Castel. Who knows you might like it," Clara stated. Clara was the top party planner in the city. She was also the cattiest. Often times losing business because of her nosey ways, but she always got her customers back because of her custom quality materials. Mirah put her trust in Clara to plan Castel's baby shower, because for the money she planned on spending, she wanted nothing else but the best and she knew Clara would deliver.

"Forget it Clara. When she doesn't like something she doesn't like it. Let's look at something else," Mirah suggested.

Clara frowned her face and continued to look through her decorations. "Well that was the last shade of green I have Mirah," Clara said with a snarl.

"Well good. Now we can look at the colors that I originally wanted. I need the softest pinks with the purest whites and the most gorgeous gold you have," Castel told her, as she flipped through the pages of Clara's design book.

"Do you really need all those colors Castel?" Mirah questioned.

"Absolutely. It's pretty and elegant like me," Castel expressed, flipping her hair. Clara rolled her eyes. "Oh, yeah, and I want those colors for my maternity shoot because they have to go on the invitations. I want everyone to see how photogenic I still am; no matter how pregnant or bloated I've become." Castel finished, rubbing her belly. Mirah smiled at her daughter's enthusiasm. She loved seeing her in good spirits.

Clara sat in the back with an annoyed look on her face. She started digging in her bag for invitation ideas. She cleared her throat. "Well, since you have a pretty good idea of what you want let's go ahead and look at the invitations now, shall we?" Clara said, placing a bigger book on Mirah's lap that read *The Ultimate Invite*.

The furry purple lining hurt Castel's eyes. "I'm suppose to find my perfect invitation in this?" Castel asked.

Clara resented her tone. "Only if you want your 'perfect' invitation to actually show some kind of class," Clara snipped. Mirah cut her eyes as Clara's cattiness began to show.

"What do you mean 'some kind of class?'" Castel questioned, fixing her body to face Clara.

"I mean, the pure elegant charm that I bring to my many functions will only do so much for this one. Let's be honest, you're talking about bringing elegance to *teen pregnancy*. There is hardly anything charming about that," Clara sneered.

"Excuse you Clara. I don't believe we asked you for your personal opinion," Mirah chimed in. "I'm paying you to plan a party, not be a family counselor."

"But see that's what I'm saying, look how you're enabling her. *You're* paying for the party. I've been talking to the two of you for the last two weeks and not once have either of you mentioned the father. Where is his contribution? Will he even be part of your 'glowing' maternity shoot?" she continued.

"Clara!" Mirah shouted.

Clara shut her mouth instantly, taken back my Mirah's tone. Castel swallowed hard as she sat tensely in her seat. She very much wanted to punch Clara in the chest regardless of the fact that she was almost seven months pregnant.

"You need to know your place Clara. I told you, I'm not paying you to criticize my daughter and what I do for her. Now, you either understand that or I find someone else. There are other planners who create quality events, even if they aren't considered the best in town," Mirah assured her.

Clara rolled her eyes and turned around, pretending to search through her decorations. The last thing she needed was another client dropping her. Mirah sucked her teeth and turned her attention to Castel who was staring holes into Clara's head. Mirah reached out to give Castel one of her gentle touches to calm her, but Castel stopped her hand. She got up and walked upstairs. Mirah let out a low sigh.

"What's wrong with her?" Clara asked. Mirah gave her a look of death. Clara shrunk back.

Upstairs, Castel locked herself in her room. She sat on the floor of her bedroom, trying to remove Clara's hateful words from her mind. The harder she tried, the louder the thoughts became in her head. Each word Clara spoke replayed in her head over and over again. It made her blood boil. She was so tired of the judgment; not just from Clara, but everyone in town. Everywhere she went she got stares, whispers, and smart remarks. She was officially over the negativity and just wanted everyone to mind their own business. She knew she was a teen mom, but she refused to believe that her life was over.

Castel caught a knot in her throat as she forced herself not to cry. She swallowed hard and let out a salty sigh. She looked at herself in the full-sized mirror hanging on her wall. She could hardly recognize herself with all the hideous swelling. The sight started to piss her off again when she felt small taps in her midsection. The movement took her by surprise. Her baby girl was never up this time of the day.

"Did I wake you?" Castel spoke to her delicate belly. "Mommy's sorry love. Mommy's sorry. I'm just tired of everyone talking about me... talking about you. Everyone wants to put their two cents in and I'm over it," Castel continued. "You know, I didn't want you like this. I always thought, when I finally had my sweet baby girl, your father and I would be married. I'd be finished with school and he would be one of the top players in the NFL. He was never sure of what team he wanted to play for. He just always knew it would be the one who offered him the most amount of money." Castel let out a little chuckle. "That's your daddy for you. Always thinking about the money." She chuckled again, but the cloud of sorrow continued to hover over her. "Man I wish he was here with us… he should be here with us!" She banged her fist on her thigh and clenched her teeth at the thought of Dante missing out on their daughter's life.

Castel stood up, rubbing the area on her thigh that she had hit. She walked over to the custom pink and gold crib near her window and ran her fingers down the engraving. It read "Mahogany." The color of Castel's cheerleading uniform. "I'm going to give you everything sweetie. All the love my parents did their best to show me and all the love that was stolen." She spoke directly to her belly with a giddy voice. "You'll never worry about getting love from anyone. I'll give you all the love you need," she finished with the smile of a cheshire cat on her face. Castel wrapped her arms around her daughter the best she could and envisioned herself finally holding sweet Mahogany in her arms. The image made her tingle.

"Castel!" Mirah shouted from downstairs, dragging Castel back to reality. Castel scoffed as she stood still, pretending she didn't hear. "Castel! Castel!" Mirah screamed louder.

Castel grunted and stomped out her room to the stairs to see what was so important. "How can I be of service?" she asked, sarcastically. She then noticed a frazzled Clara standing against the wall looking down, but Castel could not see what she was looking at. Mirah stood at the bottom of the stairs looking in the same direction. Castel made her way down to the first floor slowly, keeping her eyes on her mother. "Mom?" she questioned quietly, as she got closer to her.

Mirah moved to the side to let Castel through. Castel turned around slowly. There on the ground was Cherry, bloody and barely conscious. Castel moved cautiously toward her. The sight of Cherry's disheveled body was far from shocking for her. In truth, Castel felt nothing.

"Are you just going to look at her?" Clara broke out of her frightened state. "You can't just leave her bleeding on your floor. It'll stain," Clara told them.

"I'll call John," Mirah spoke.

"Who dropped her off here?" Castel asked.

"I don't know. I opened the door to see Clara off and there she was leaning up against my car," Mirah explained.

"Well put her back outside and leave the neighbors to find her. Or better yet, some stray dogs." The animosity in Castel's voice was thick.

"Castel!" Mirah couldn't believe her daughter's harshness.

"I hope you're a better mother than you are a friend." Clara chimed in.

"Shut up Clara!" Castel snapped. "Put her back outside Mom. I don't care about any help she needs. She can sit here and die for all I care, but we're not calling my father to get her out of another stupid situation. She'll have to learn how to take care of herself and be loyal to those who look out for her when she's in hell." Castel stormed back up the stairs, but Mirah was right behind her. She grabbed Castel by the arm and turned her back around.

"You have lost your mind," Mirah told her. "Call John on the house phone, Clara. Tell him what's going on," Mirah demanded. She turned her attention back to Castel. "We are not going to leave this helpless little girl here Castel. At least help me get her onto the couch so I can clean her up," Mirah pleaded.

"Little girl?" Castel could not believe her mother. "This idiot druggie is far from a little girl. She wasn't a little girl when she humiliated me in front of my entire cheer team that I got her on. She wasn't a little girl when she insulted me for being pregnant!" Castel was angrier than she'd ever been. Mirah could see the flames brewing over her. "I don't care what happens to her. I'm done trying to help her. Like I said, let the dogs help her," Castel finished, snatching her arm away from her mother.

"Castel Jean!!" Mirah called one more time, but Castel ignored her and continued to her room where she slammed the door behind her as hard as she could. Mirah scoffed in disappointment at her daughter's anger. She turned and looked at Clara in the doorway, still on the phone. Mirah swallowed hard. "Is John coming?" she stammered.

"He's not answering, but I'll keep calling." Clara replied in an unusually timid voice.

"Ok. Can you please help me get her to the couch?" Mirah asked, softly. Clara gave her a slight smile, put the phone on speaker, and together they picked up Cherry and placed her on the sofa.

"Do you want me to get a towel?" Clara asked.

Mirah kept her eyes on Cherry, moving her messy hair from her face. Cherry's upper lip was cut and both eyes were bruised and swollen. Gentle tears fell from Mirah's eyes onto Cherry's dirty cheeks.

"I wonder who did this to her?" Clara's spoke again, hovering over Mirah's shoulder.

"She did," Mirah explained, wiping the tears from her cheeks. "Can you get me that towel now?"

Clara gave Mirah a soft smile and rubbed her on the back and then went to get a wet towel. Mirah leaned over Cherry staring at her with a mother's pain in her eyes. She remembered the first time she saw Cherry. It was during Castel's freshman year and Cherry had been sitting by herself on the benches outside of the school. Castel noticed her as she was getting out of the car and asked Mirah if she could say hi to her. It was such a proud moment for Mirah to see that her talks of treating others with kindness had really paid off. They walked over to Cherry together and as bubbly as can be Castel said hi and offered to share her bagel with her. Cherry looked up at both Mirah and Castel puzzled. She hesitated for a while before giving them a slight smile and accepted Castel's offer. Mirah never forgot that day. She always remembered that look of uncertainty in Cherry's eyes, as if she was tired of the world misleading her. As the years passed Cherry became her surrogate daughter, even though she never told her. Anytime something happened with Cherry, Mirah felt obligated to see her through it and this time was no different. Mirah inhaled deeply and held her tears back. She then stood up to reposition Cherry on the sofa.

Clara returned with the towel, soaking in a crystal bowl she gotten from the kitchen. She placed it on the floor next to Mirah. "I tried to get Castel to come back downstairs. She is the stubborn one, you know?" Clara sneered.

"She gets it from her mother." Mirah replied, cutting her eyes at Clara.

Clara rolled her eyes. "Are you going to call her parents or something? Someone has to be worried about her."

Mirah let out a long sigh as she finished positioning Cherry. "Nope. We are her family. Well, the closest she'll let anybody get to family. Can I have the towel now?"

Clara leaned down, squeezed the water from the towel, being very careful to not get it on rug, and handed it to Mirah. Mirah kneeled down and carefully wiped the drying blood from Cherry's lip. Cherry flinched softly, but Mirah continued wiping her cheeks and delicately patting her eyes. The more she looked at Cherry's bruises the more knots formed in her stomach.

Clara noticed Mirah shaking. She stepped closer and grabbed Mirah's hand. "I got this. You go and check on Castel."

Mirah swallowed hard and then gave Clara a smile. "Thank you," she expressed, patting Clara's hand. "Can you try John again? When you get a chance…please?" Mirah's eyes were still on Cherry.

Clara nodded her head and took the towel. Mirah headed upstairs. Her steps were slow and light. She could feel the troubles of her family weighing her down as she dragged herself to Castel's door. She listened for a moment, but there was only silence. Slowly, she opened the door and peeked her head in. There, on the floor, was Castel, sitting in front of her bed with her journal.

"Castel… I need you to talk to me. What has gotten into you?" Mirah asked, knowing the answer. Castel continued to sit quietly. Mirah stepped all the way in and closed the door. "Clara is helping me with Cherry… she hasn't woken up yet though. We're going to have to take her to the hospital," Mirah continued. She moved closer to Castel and sat down next to her. She stared at the side of her daughter's face and noticed the dry tear stains on her cheek. She reached out her hand to touch Castel, but she put her hands up.

"Leave me alone, Mom. I don't want to deal with this. I don't want to deal with *her*," Castel admitted.

Mirah paused as she continued to stare at the side of Castel's face. "This is not you sweetheart. This is not the young lady I've raised for the last sixteen years. What happened to that girl who always treated others with respect and kindness?" Mirah asked, firmly.

Castel gave her mother a sharp look. "*That girl* was taken advantage of. *That girl* was treated with disrespect and played by the very people who swore they would always have her back." Castel's voice began to break. "*That girl,* Mom… is no more. I am tired of being treated unfairly. Look at me! Look at what being kind to others has gotten me." Castel's voice intensified. Mirah sat in silence, looking at the pain gushing from her daughter's eyes. "This isn't supposed to happen to me. Not me," Castel cried.

Mirah opened her mouth to give her usual words of encouragement, but her throat was empty. There was nothing. Her daughter's tears dripped off her chin and her pain filled the room but there wasn't a single word she could give to ease Castel's pain.

Mirah's silence gave Castel the hardest slap of reality. This was her life. Nothing she did and no words from her mother would change that. The thought washed over her like a river and in her mother's arms she dropped and sobbed viciously. Mirah wrapped her arms around her as tightly as she could as warm tears trickled down her cheek.

REALITY

Dante paced back and forth from his room to the bathroom. He grunted and stomped as thoughts swallowed his skull. "No. No. No. This is a lie. It has to be a lie. Not me. This can't be happening to me," Dante spoke out loud with his hands clasping his head.

He walked back into his room and dropped down beside his bed. It was already a full two weeks since he got the news he was HIV positive and every day that went by, a piece of his sanity went with it. He refused to believe the results even though he got a second opinion from his physician that also came back positive.

Dante sat on his floor staring at himself in the full length mirror hanging on the wall. His shrinking frame was too much for him to bare. The blotches on his skin made him cringe. His once long, thick, locs were now dry and full of breakage. He hardly recognized himself and the sight angered him. Dante jumped off the floor and charged at the mirror, kicking it with all his might. The glass shattered everywhere, covering the carpet. Dante just stood in the middle of his room looking at the floor.

"What is wrong with you now?" Brian's voice traveled from the doorway.

Dante continued to look at the ground. The last thing he wanted to do at this moment was face his dad. Brian gave a look of confusion and then exhaled aggressively as he walked in and laid some papers on Dante's bed.

"Whatever your problem is, this is not the time to deal with it. We have bigger things to handle." Dante rolled his eyes at his dad's insensitivity. "I set you up with some classes downtown... bartending courses. The girls at the club gave me the info," he expressed, as he continued to sort out the papers. Dante turned his head slightly to his father. ""I think it'll do you some good to start doing something productive instead of moping around this house. I mean, if you can't be the star football player we worked for…at least you can get into the family business. Get your bank account up some way…right?" Brian finished and turned toward Dante.

Dante was still in his stance amid the broken glass. Part of him couldn't believe his father and the other part was far from shocked. Brian never missed an opportunity to make money off of Dante.

Brian leaned in to Dante, perplexed that he was still standing uncertain.

"Hello? What's wrong with you? Get over here and look at these papers," Brian demanded.

"I don't want to look at those paper and I definitely don't plan to be someone's bartender!" Dante finally spoke up. "Why can't you just leave me alone? Can't you see I don't want to be bothered? Can't you just respect what I want for once? Man, I'm so tired of you!" Dante expressed, with his body now facing his father.

Brian rolled his eyes and looked at Dante with disbelief. "What *you've* always wanted has done nothing, but destroy you!"

"No! What you've wanted for me has done nothing but destroy me! Look at me! Look at what all your nagging and nonsense has turned me into!" Dante screamed, as tears swelled up in his eyes. His built up frustration finally started to boil over.

"The weight you lost must clearly be messing with your brain," Brian insulted, which only made Dante's stomach cramp further. "I didn't do anything to you but push you to be your best. *You* love football. I put you in football camp since the age of seven. You love those stupid little girls who bring you nothing but drama. I show you how to be a player like your father," Brian admitted with a chuckle. "You love to party and drink. I'm going to introduce you to the club life by being a bartender! Now get over here and fill out these forms." He turned and looked through what papers he wanted Dante to sign first. Dante balled up his fist as he stared his father down from the back. Brian's arrogance annoyed him more than anything else in this world. Brian turned to see Dante's hands formed into fist. He gave a small smirk and dropped the papers on the ground.

"You feeling like the Champ? Take your best shot," Brian ordered. He stretched his arms out and waited for Dante to charge.

Dante felt his palms start to sweat. He couldn't take his father out at his best football weight so he knew he would be no match for him now. Dante weighed his options, thinking of all the possible ways he could take his father out, but then a wave of guilt and shame swept over him. Was he really going to fight his own father? It was different when Brian would beat him. Then he was just being a parent. This was him antagonizing his own dad. Dante unclenched his fists and relaxed his body.

Brian smiled. "I knew you couldn't do it! Never man enough to take on a real man. You probably wore the dress in that relationship with Princess too. That's why she has your life all screwed up now." Brian taunted Dante.

Dante couldn't believe his ears. He became enraged and threw punches at Brian with all his might, but wasn't quick enough. Brian dodged each punch with ease and his quickness caused Dante to lose his balance. Brian gave him one fierce blow to the face and Dante dropped to the ground. Blood gushed from his busted lip as he hit the floor. Brian walked over and stood over him. An urge to kick his son came over him, but quickly went away as a tear rolled down the side of Dante's face. Brian felt knots squeeze his stomach as his son began to cry, motionless on the ground. He shook off his anger and went to the bathroom to get a towel. Dante rolled over on his side to try and get himself off the floor. He wiped his lip and stared at the ruby blood on his hand. The sight shot reality through his body.

"Oh no," he thought, remembering he still hadn't told his dad about his deadly disease.

Brian came from behind and reached down to wipe the blood off his son's lip, but Dante jerked away with haste and jumped off the ground. He wiped the blood from his hand on his pants and used his shirt to cover his lip. Brian continued behind him. "Dante let me help," Brian pleaded.

"Leave me alone. I can do it myself," Dante demanded. Dante stumbled into the bathroom and ran the hot water, quickly trying to rinse his mouth. Brian refused to stop forcing his help. He grabbed Dante by the back of the neck struggling to wipe his face. Dante was stricken with fear as he looked at his dad's hand get closer to the HIV blood on his face. He pushed his father with brute strength and Brian stumbled, almost hitting the wall. He turned and looked at Dante who was trembling with panic, uneasily covering his mouth.

A perplexed Brian stared at his son. "What's wrong with you?" Brian asked, with the most sincerity Dante had ever heard in his father's voice. He took one step closer to Dante, but his son leaned back trying not to fall in the shower. "Why don't you want me to touch you, Dante?" Brian asked again.

Dante looked at the ground still holding his hand over his wet, bloody mouth. "Please… just leave me," Dante begged softly through his fingers.

"Dante…" Brian began, still moving toward him. Dante circled around the bathroom, away from his father. "What is going on with you?" Brian asked one more time, with fear lingering behind his words.

Dante felt a boulder fill his throat. The fright in his spirit stopped any more tears from falling. He knew this was it. He had to say something. He couldn't hold it in anymore. He slowly turned to look at his father who continued to stare at him. Brian's eyes were filled with something Dante had never seen before — concern. He cleared his throat and let his words roll off of his tongue slowly. "I…have…H…I…V."

Brian's ears rang. The room began to spin as his son's words hit him. He stumbled back and dropped against the wall, sinking to the floor. Dante cautiously stepped towards him. Brian looked up at him with a blank stare. "No. You can't. They're wrong. The doctor. The test…it's wrong," Brian said, in a hushed voice.

Dante shook his head. "No, it's not. I got tested twice. I have it… I have it," Dante admitted. His words drifted off.

Silence hovered over them. Brian put his hands in his face and let out a loud grunt. "Didn't I always tell you to use protection?" Brian screamed, picking up his head to look at Dante. Dante froze at his dad's sudden anger. "I always told you to use freaking condoms! You never listen! Now look at you! Look at what you've done to yourself!" Brian scolded.

The boulder in Dante's throat dropped to his stomach. He felt his knees go weak. "Dad…I…" Dante tried to defend himself, but his words were lost.

The look of sheer disgust on Brian's face ate away at the leftovers of Dante's damaged spirit. Brian shook his head, no longer wanting to waste his time staring at the disappointment he was forced to have as a son. He picked himself up off the floor. Dante reached to help him with his clean hand.

"Don't touch me!" Brian shouted. "Don't you dare put your AIDS fingers on me!" he continued.

"Dad, it's not AIDS. It's HIV," Dante cried.

"SAME THING! Where do you think the AIDS comes from...or were you too stupid to understand that too?" Brian insulted. Dante felt the last of his spirit be devoured by his father's words. "Nothing! That's what you are to me now! Absolutely nothing! What good are you now? What can anyone do with you now? What a waste of eighteen years of my life!" Brian spit.

Dante hung his head with his father's shame. Brian turned and left the room. He stomped downstairs and out of the house, slamming the door so hard the entire place shook. Dante continued to stand in the bathroom. His eyes were shut tight as he did his best to clear his father's words from his head. He imagined the good times with his dad. Moments where they were both proud. Dante let out a small smile at visions of them watching the Falcons on Sunday and Brian cheering him on during his games as a child. For a moment, Dante began to feel better, but it was short lived. Dante grit his teeth and squeezed his eyes closed. Brian's voice got louder and louder the more he tried to clear it out. The boulder dropped from his stomach and tears slowly released from his eyes. Alone and empty he whispered, "Sorry."

DIMINISHED

Castel joyfully bobbed down the hallway of the Phipps Plaza. She was determined to get out of her funky mood and she couldn't think of a better way than shopping for her and Mahogany. $2000 and ten bags later, her mood was a hundred times better. She stopped at Johnny Rockets to get them something to eat. After all, shopping is very energy consuming.

She looked at the menu inquisitively, as if it was the most important decision of her life.

"Everything is so good, it's always hard to decide, huh?" A man whispered from behind her.

Castel turned around, ready to give a rude remark, and saw Josh standing behind her. Her face lit up. "Hey you!" she expressed, embracing him with a huge hug. "I didn't expect to see you for a long time, what with all your great success and all," she told him.

Josh blushed. He couldn't help but be proud of his amazing success and it was nice that someone, who knew him before it all, was so genuinely happy. "Well, you know me Cas. I never saw failure as an option." He beamed.

"Absolutely. How those Hawks treating you?" she inquired.

"Pretty good. You know, I still have to lay my oats, but I'm determined to gain my respect." He pounded his chest.

"Don't hurt yourself," she said sarcastically. They both let out a good laugh.

"So what's been up with you? I see pregnancy is doing you good. You're still as beautiful as ever. I can't wait to meet little Mahogany," he expressed, rubbing her belly.

Castel smiled at his positivity. "Thanks Josh. Lord knows we've been through too much," she said, rolling her eyes.

Josh gave a face of sympathy. "How has Dante been acting in the last few months? When I saw him a while back, he did say it was really stressful," Josh admitted.

"*He's* stressed out? Yeah right! I bet it's really stressful distancing yourself to wallow in self pity, instead of celebrating your child," Castel scoffed, folding her arms.

"I'm sorry. I didn't mean to upset you. I just thought you guys were on better terms by now. My fault," he told her.

Castel relaxed. "You're good. I'm just over his nonsense. Whatever he wants to do with himself at this point he can. I'm through with him." The disappointment in her voice was heavy.

"Don't feel bad. I understand where you're coming from. Once I found out about Cherry and him, I was through too." Josh's words dropped from his lips like rocks.

Castel stood in confusion. She leaned in closer. "What do you mean him and Cherry?" she questioned.

Josh gave her a look of uncertainty. He hesitated, but then spoke, "You know? They were messing around. He slipped up one day and told me. I was destroyed and confronted Cherry, but you know how she is. She never admits when she is wrong. I…" Josh broke off when he realized the shock on Castel's face. He bit his lip as an awkward silence stretched between them. "Cas?" Josh finally spoke, breaking her trance.

"I'm sorry." Her voice cracked. "I…I just…" she stammered.

"No… it's not you. I didn't know I would be sharing all this new information." Josh joked trying to ease the tension.

"It's OK. I mean, I can't be all that shocked. They never really cared about me anyway." She laughed nervously. Josh looked down at the ground. "Hey don't be like that. I'll be fine." Castel assured him, placing her hand on his shoulder.

He looked back at her forcing a smile. He felt so bad for her. There was so much pain under such a pretty face. With nothing else left to say, they embraced in one last hug before parting to go their own ways.

Once she was clear of his sight, Castel rushed as fast as she could to her car. She shoved her bags in the backseat of her BMW, jumped in the driver seat, and raced out the parking lot. "Those jerks. Those stupid, ungrateful jerks. No wonder she was never happy for me. No wonder she hated my baby. All her lies!" Castel shouted, doing seventy down the highway. "How could I be so stupid? That's why Dante had the nerve to accuse me of sleeping around. This was all a game!"

She pulled in the driveway of Dante's house and sat for a minute to let her temper simmer down. Gently, she got out her car and walked to the back of the house. She moved cunningly, retrieving the spare key from under the black flowerpot with the sunflower growing in it. Sunflowers were Dante's favorite flower. She slowly opened the door and walked into the hallway. All the lights were off and the house was lit with lavender and vanilla candles. Castel felt sick. The only time candles were ever lit in the house was when Dante wanted to be romantic.

Castel took a deep breath and stomped upstairs. Pregnant or not, she was ready to fight Dante and any whore he was laying with. She secretly hoped it was Cherry so she could kill two birds with one stone. She got to his door and paused as she prepared herself for what she was going to see. She then opened the door with haste. There, on the bed was a frail Dante sleeping alone. She walked over and stood next to him. She wanted to punch him as hard as her pregnant body would let her. She imagined herself ripping each one of his limbs off his body and cooking them slowly. She looked frantically around the room searching for anything to throw at him or hit him with. Nothing. Nothing that would give the impact she wanted. She turned around and went to the bathroom. There on the floor was a clear blue bucket, she filled it with cold water and pushed it back to Dante's room. With all the strength she possessed she picked up the loaded bucket and poured all the water on Dante's bare weak body.

Gasping for air, Dante jumped out of his sleep. Gagging and coughing, he did his best to compose himself. Finally aware of his surroundings, he looked toward his door to see Castel with his bath bucket at her feet. "What the heck is wrong with you?" Dante asked through his coughs.

"How dare you sleep with her?" Castel roared.

"What? What are you talking about?" He coughed. "Does it look like I'm sleeping with anyone?" Dante shouted, banging his head to get the water out of his ears.

"I don't mean now you idiot. I mean then...before. How dare you?" she yelled again.

"I don't know what you're talking about you psycho! How did you even get in my house?" Dante questioned as he slowly got up out of his bed.

Castel circled around following him. "Cherry? Of all the filth on this earth...Cherry is who you cheated on me with?" she finally said.

Dante looked at her with no remorse and spoke, "You're about a year too late don't you think?" His voice was cold.

Castel felt a stab in her heart. "You suck. You absolutely suck. After you had the nerve to deny my child and call me a whore — "

"Please, Cas. Don't even bother to waste your breath. I don't care and I don't want to hear it, so get out." Dane gestured to the door.

"I'm not going anywhere. You're finally going to answer me. *This time...* you are going to answer to me," she demanded.

Dante scoffed and grabbed a t-shirt from his desk chair to wipe the leftover beads of water off his face before walking toward the door. He brushed past Castel, but she was hot on his heels.

"You are so selfish," she cried.

"Tell me something I don't know," Dante admitted.

"This isn't fair. I loved you and this is how you repay me, Dante. You cheated on me with someone who I believed was my best friend. You lied to me and denied my child... our child. Our daughter should have both parents in her life," Castel scolded.

Dante stopped to face her. "Last time I checked, you had both parents and still came out screwed up. I had just my dad and was even worse. Probably, with just a mom in her life, she'll have a better chance." He made his way down the stairs slowly, almost missing the last step.

"Dante please. This isn't right. She doesn't deserve this kind of life."

Dante paused at Castel's words. He turned back around and moved towards her. Castel held her breath. "She doesn't deserve 'this kind of life?' And why not? Huh? Why doesn't she deserve 'this kind of life' Castel? Huh?" he asked her in a low frightening voice. Castel continued to stand quietly as Dante continued. "What does one do to deserve the 'kind of life' where your parents always throw you off to the side? What does one do to deserve the 'kind of life' where you can bust your behind all your life and still have everything you've worked for ripped right from under you?" Dante's voice got shaky. "What did I do to deserve this? I am the best player that school has ever seen and yet look at me? Look what I've become?" he cried. Tears welled up in Castel's eyes for him. "I was suppose to have it all, but all I ended up with is defeat and this stupid HIV." The slip of his tongue caught him by surprise.

Dante put his arms down and backed away from Castel. Castel's lip quivered. The thickest knot swelled up in her throat. She opened her mouth, but no words came out. Dante puts his face in his hands and began to cry softly. Castel looked on with pity. She couldn't help but feel sorry for Dante. Despite all the pain he caused her, she wanted to comfort him. She hesitated for a minute, but then moved closer to console him. As she grabbed his shoulders and stroked him gently, he shook her off.

"Please... please go. I just want to be alone," he expressed.

"No. You don't have to be. Let me help," Castel begged.

"There isn't anything you can do for me. My life is over Cas. I'm done. Even my dad gave up on me," he admitted, hanging his head.

"Dante... I'm still here. Our Daughter... She'll be here — "

"Stop Castel." He cut her off.

"Please Dante."

"Get out!" he shouted.

"No. I can't." Her resilience angered him. He grunted and balled up his fist. Castel backed away. He punched the wall and began knocking over the stands with the lit candles. "Dante! Stop!" Castel shrieked.

He turned to her and charged. Castel ran for the living room as quick as she could, but he followed, pushing the furniture aside and knocking over more candles. They rolled on the floor to the long burgundy curtains hanging on the window. The curtains burst into flames. A hysterical Castel stood in the corner by the fireplace looking at the rippling flames shoot up the wall. She brought her attention back to Dante who stood just several feet away from her, huffing like a bull. His eyes were bloodshot. Castel was paralyzed with fear. She was stuck between a lunatic and a fire. Dante balled up his fist and raised his hand to strike her. In a panic Castel picked up the poker that was leaning against the fireplace and lunged at Dante, stabbing him in the chest. His crimson blood oozed down the poker. Castel stood in shock still holding her weapon. Dante stumbled back and dropped to the ground. Castel let go of the poker and began to cry, looking over Dante's body.

"No... Baby... no," she cried.

Her tears fell but the smoke from the fire burned her eyes. Castel gathered herself and stepped over Dante. She went to his feet and tried pulling him across the floor, but he still weighed too much for her to move. The smoke became thicker and Castel began to gag. She glanced over one more time at Dante's dying body.

"I'm sorry. ...I'm so sorry," she sobbed.

She gently stroked his leg one last time and turned to rush out the door. She closed her eyes tight as she worked the locks, fighting to get out. Finally she turned the last lock, swung the door open, and stumbled onto the lawn. She dropped to her knees and coughed the smoke out of her lungs. She wiped her eyes with her shirt, trying to regain her vision. She heard voices screaming around her and sirens blasting in the distance.

"Get me some water and a towel honey," a woman's voice yelled. "It's OK, Dear. You're OK," the woman told Castel. She leaned Castel back on the grass, rubbing her face to remove the soot.

Castel whimpered. "I'm sorry," she tells the woman, as she gasps for air.

"No, Dear. It's OK. We just have to make sure you and your baby are alright," The woman assured her, as a man finally brought her a bowl with a towel soaking in it. She placed the cold towel over Castel's eyes, patting it gently. The cool water was refreshing to Castel. The woman removed the towel from her face. Castel opened her eyes to see an elderly woman hovering over her. "Is that better?" the woman asked. Castel nodded her head, but the woman gave Castel a concerned look and leaned in closer. "What happened?" she asked.

Castel looked in a daze. She turned her head toward the house. Flames shot through the roof and around the house. Smoke filled the air. She couldn't believe her eyes.

"Was there anyone else in the house?" the man asked.

Castel remembered Dante's lifeless body on the living room floor. Bittersweet tears dropped from her eyes. She turned her head back to the woman. "All I wanted was for us to be a family. I just wanted us to be happy," Castel said, crying harder.

The elderly couple looked at each other and then back at Castel. The woman pulled her in close and held her tight in the middle of the lawn.

Firefighters surrounded Brian's crisp house. The police began taping off the area to secure it, as Castel looked on from the police car. The handcuffs dug into her swollen wrists and she fidgeted in the back seat staring at the huge crowd of bystanders. She eyeballed the police officers working the scene, wondering if she would see her dad. She hung her head and closed her eyes. She hopelessly wanted this all to be a dream. She envisioned herself back at home in her bed with her feet up and Dante sitting next to her. In the vision, everything was the way it should be.

"Move! Get out of my way!" a man shouted. The voice was all too familiar. Castel turned her head to see Brian pushing through the crowd. "What the heck happened to my house?" Brian yelled at the police officers standing closest to him.

"Are you the owner of this house?" an officer asked.

"That's what I just said. Now tell me what the heck happened to my house," Brain demanded.

The officer moved closer. "We received a call regarding a house fire and when we finally put it out we discovered the body of what appears to be a young man," the officer tells him quietly. Brian gave him a look of disbelief. "Please…if you can… I'd like you to come with me to the hospital to identify the body." The officer lifted up the tape for Brian to cross.

Brian moved slowly, following behind the officer. As they got closer to the car other police officials exited the house with the body on a stretcher. Brian's heart dropped and he rushed over to the body, pushing the officials aside to unzip the bag. There was Dante. Dead. Most of his face was burned, but Brian still recognized his son. A prickling pain ran through Brian's body. Shaking, he reached out to touch his son's face, but the officer stopped him.

"Please sir. You can't touch him. She informed us he was HIV positive," the officer told him.

Brian turned to look at the officer with perplexity. "Who is she? Who told you that?" he questioned. The officer pointed in the direction of the police car. There was Castel staring in their direction. Brian became irate. "You did this? You! This is all your fault," he hollered, moving towards the car that Castel had been placed in.

"Sir..." the officer called, but Brian could not hear him over his anger.

"You killed my son! Are you happy? Are you?" he screamed.

The officers grabbed him and pulled him to the ground to restrain him. Castel looked away. She turned her attention to the other side to see Josh standing in the crowd. They locked eyes. Josh's eyes were filled with sorrow. She shook her head at him, not wanting him to feel sorry for her. She gave him a slight smile. He gave her a nod. Tears started to swell up in her eyes, but she refused to let them fall. She leaned her head back and rested it on the seat, trying to clear her mind, but she heard her mother's gentle voice calling her name. At first, she thought she was hearing things, but then it was followed by her father's voice. She sat up and turned around to see her parents at the back of the police car.

"Stand down, Officer," John demanded, but the officer refused.

"Sorry Chief. I can't let you through. Protocol….you understand. You have to meet us at the station," the officer informed him.

John was in shock. He looked back at Mirah, who was still looking at Castel. Castel stared at her mother, as she began to cry. "Forgive me," she mouthed to her mom.

The officers jumped in the front seats and started the car. They drove off, heading for the police station. Castel kept her eyes on her parents as they faded behind her. The tears she tried so hard to fight back, finally fell from her eyes. She watched as the dreams she once craved, diminish away.

CONCLUSION

After all the smoke cleared and the ashes blew away, the traumatizing pain of betrayal, lies, and deception swallowed them all. The pain ate away at the dreams they told their hearts they once desired, leaving emptiness, but who is to say they can't be healed? How can one reach their fullest potential if they are never knocked down? It is how and when they choose to stand back up that determines if they can save what has been...diminished.

THROUGH THE PAIN

"Alrighty little lady, time to move it," the guard ordered.

"Where am I going? My court date isn't today," Castel said.

"You have a visitor," she responded, sarcastically.

Castel gave her a peculiar look as she got up off her bed. The creak of her cell door scrapped her eardrums. The masculine female guard roughly placed the cold metal cuffs on Castel's tiny wrist. She was relieved the swelling had finally started to go down. The walls of the Metro State Prison reeked of pain, agony, and disappointment as they made their way through the cell block. To Castel, it was no different than the life she once knew.

Castel scanned the visiting area, and rolled her eyes at a table in the corner. There, dressed all in black like she was in mourning, sat Mirah. Walking toward her, Castel realized she shouldn't be surprised by her mother's cliche behavior. She had always had a flair for the dramatic.

Castel sat down slowly, but took a moment to gaze at the other inmates and their visitors. They all looked so pleased to have their loved ones visiting them. The hope for freedom beamed through their eyes. Castel had zero interest in that hope. Hope failed her a long time ago.

"How long are you going to act as if I'm not sitting here?" Mirah spit out. Castel gave another eye roll and stared at her reflection in Mirah's glasses.

"Do you have to wear those *every* time you come visit me? It's embarrassing."

"Excuse me? The only thing embarrassing is the fact that I have to be here at all. Besides, I am a well-known doctor; I can't risk anyone actually seeing me in a jailhouse," Mirah said in a hush. "Did you ever think about that? This has been extremely hard for your father and me. We are doing the best we can. You could at least be a little more grateful," Mirah's tone increased.

"It's been hard for you? Seriously mom?" Castel scoffed and looked away. Mirah's guilt dug into her skin.

They sat in silence for a few minutes before Mirah started again. "Mahogany started moving her head this week. The doctors are excited for her progress."

Castel's body tingled. Her anger almost made her forget about her baby girl. After all the stress she put her body through Mahogany had been born premature at three and half pounds, with water on her brain and serious respiratory problems. Castel was just grateful her daughter's heart was still beating. Her mother's news was the breath of fresh air she needed after these long two months. "Is she out of her incubator yet?" Castel finally asked.

"No no. Not yet. It's still too early for that… but I am hopeful." Mirah assured, with a smile. Castel returned the gesture and then leaned in closer. "Has Brian ever come to see her?"

Mirah's faced dropped. "Absolutely not, and he better not step any where near the hospital, or I'll make sure John rips his black heart out." Mirah snatched away from Castel.

Castel understood her mother's anger, but she still wanted Brian to be part of Mahogany's life in remembrance of Dante. She swallowed hard. "Mom… please?"

"Don't you dare beg me to let that demon see my grandchild." Mirah cut her off. "After he wished death on her *and* you! Now you so stupidly want me to put Mahogany in danger by letting him come near her. Oh, I don't think so," Mirah scolded, crossing her arms. "What you need to be more concerned about is getting through this and getting back to the people who truly love you." Castel felt a cold air cover her. Mirah looked at her daughter in disbelief. She couldn't believe Castel. "Please Cas… let's just talk about something else for now. I didn't come here to fight," Mirah pleaded and nervously began to tap her fingernails on the table. "Um... Cherry got arrested again. The girl is out of control. I'm worried about her.".

Castel's head shot up and she straightened in her seat. "You think talking about *her* won't start an argument? If you don't want to talk about Brian then we definitely will not be talking about Cherry. She's *been* out of control." Castel spit out her words. The disgust she felt still evident with every syllable.

"I'm telling you because I don't want it to be a shock once they finally transfer her here," Mirah explained.

"Transfer her here? Why exactly would they do that? Petty offenses don't come here." The curiosity in Castel's voice mounted.

"That's what I'm trying to tell you…."

"Alright! Visiting time is over," the head guard yelled out. The prisoners said their good-byes to their loved ones and walked to the door. Castel got up and followed. Mirah swallowed hard as she watched her daughter leave her one more time. It seemed each time was more painful than the last.

ABOUT THE AUTHOR

Shelby Bentil is a passionate and fearless young woman, who believes her words can change the world. She is of Ghanaian descent and was born and raised in Newark, New Jersey. Growing up in one of Newark's most deplorable housing projects, she learned that the sky is far from the limit, but the beginning of greatness. Through storytelling, Shelby opens up about her deepest and most hopeful desires, darkest days, and greatest vision. She believes you don't have to sacrifice the beauty of your soul, for the desires of your heart. With God as her provider and protector, she knows nothing is impossible. For Shelby, life is what you make of it, so you should make it beautiful!

CONNECT WITH SHELBY
ON SOCIAL MEDIA

Facebook......................... @DiminishedDreams
Instagram ....shelby_bentil
Twitter....................................... shelby_bentil
LinkedIn ....Shelby Bentil

www.ingramcontent.com/pod-product-compliance
Lightning Source LLC
Chambersburg PA
CBHW022228010526
44113CB00033B/649